Acceptance and Commitment Therapy
Workbook for Depression

Acceptance and Commitment Therapy
Workbook for Depression

Moving Beyond Depression, Embracing Your Values, and Living with Purpose

Elizabeth Weiss, PsyD

ROCKRIDGE
PRESS

First Rockridge Press trade paperback edition 2022

Rockridge Press and the Rockridge Press logo are trademarks or registered trademarks of Callisto Media Inc. and/or its affiliates in the United States and other countries and may not be used without written permission.

For general information on our other products and services, please contact our Customer Care Department within the United States at (866) 744-2665, or outside the United States at (510) 253-0500.

Paperback ISBN: 978-1-63878-745-7 | eBook ISBN: 978-1-68539-129-4

Manufactured in the United States of America

Interior and Cover Designer: Jenny Paredes
Art Producer: Janice Ackerman
Editor: Laura Cerrone
Production Editor: Jael Fogle
Production Manager: Holly Haydash

All illustrations used under license from Shutterstock.com
Author photo courtesy of Barbara Masek

10 9 8 7 6 5 4 3 2 1 0

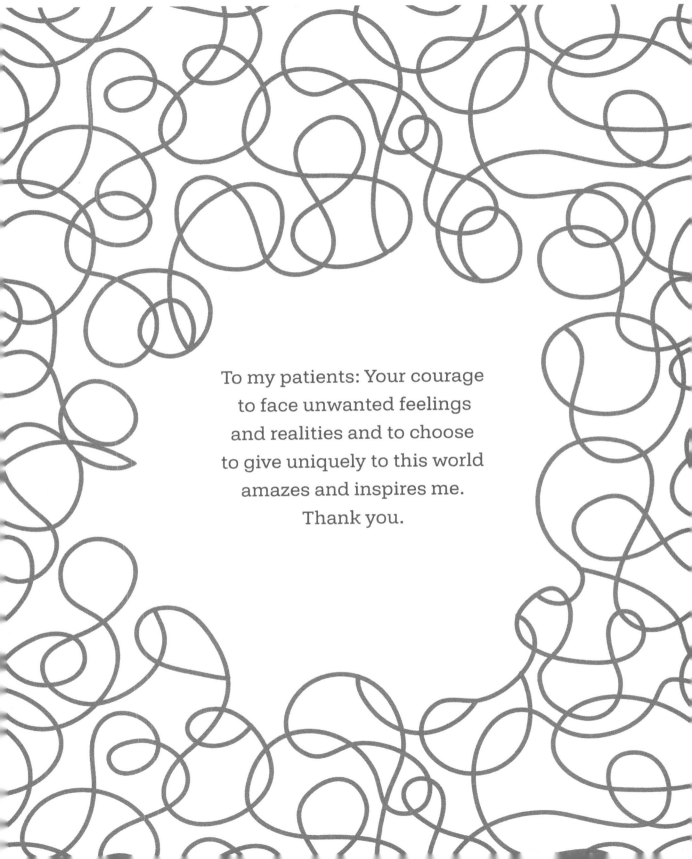

To my patients: Your courage
to face unwanted feelings
and realities and to choose
to give uniquely to this world
amazes and inspires me.
Thank you.

CONTENTS

INTRODUCTION

I learned about depression as a child. My playful, fun-loving mother would disappear and, in her place, a frightening, sad person who might yell and be mean would call herself my mother. Sometimes she would go away to hospitals and come back seeming weak and tentative, not sure what to do or how to be our mom.

Decades of medications, hospitalizations, and suicide attempts took their toll on her and the whole family. Would we children "inherit" this nightmare "disease" and live similarly compromised lives? Would she ever be free of this misery? And yet, throughout her life, there were times when the "real Mom" came back, finding ways to reconnect, apologize, and both grieve and celebrate life with us. What inexplicable transformation happened that allowed her joyous loving self to return? How could we increase the times her healthy self was present? Could we banish the thief called depression?

Depression is common, affecting approximately 5 percent of the population globally. Like most people, I witnessed its impact on friends, coworkers, and students. I tried to be supportive but sought work in areas far from mental health. Then 9/11 happened. Seeing productive, vibrant people succumb to depression after the terrorist attacks in 2001 triggered the despair I had known with my mother. I could no longer hide in the safe work of science and technology. I realized I had to face the "black dog" that stole people's health and vitality and try to make a difference. I needed to change careers. I applied to doctoral programs to become a clinical psychologist.

Nothing prepared me for the knowledge revolution that had occurred since my mother's death. The old mythology that depression was a lifetime condition requiring ongoing medication and that children of individuals with depression were destined to a similar path was being challenged. Neuroscience had demonstrated that our brains have "plasticity" and can heal. Both anatomical and clinical research explored which tools are most effective at helping people overcome depression.

The balance of the stressors and the resources we have at a given time in our lives essentially determines whether we will experience conditions such as depression. This workbook offers one approach to increasing resources. ACT is a form of behavioral therapy that combines mindfulness, self-acceptance, and values-based life. This workbook may add enough resources to use alone, but depression can derail lives in many ways. Take stock of the resources you have in place before you start using this workbook. Is your "team"—therapists, medication, structured classes or programs, supportive friends or family, supportive patterns such as exercising and socializing, workbooks—at the right level for the challenges you are facing? The Resources section at the back of the book includes ways to increase the level and types of support you have.

Depression is more treatable now than it has ever been. The skills taught in this workbook are shown to be an effective form of treatment. The first two chapters can help you decide whether this is an approach you want to begin. Best wishes to you.

HOW TO USE THIS BOOK

Acceptance and Commitment Therapy (ACT) is one of the newer treatment approaches. ACT teaches how to activate your values and strengths to overcome the power of depression. You may want to use this on your own or with a therapist or support group. You may choose to work from start to finish or choose which section or activity feels right depending on your needs and time availability.

Allowing this workbook to be a trusted companion will help you get more out of it. Write and draw in it, fold the corners of important pages, take it with you. One client described how having the anger management workbook we were using on the car seat beside them reminded them to pause before getting in a road rage altercation. The work you put into this book can help it be centering for you.

Part 1 provides an overview of depression (chapter 1) and an introduction to ACT (chapter 2). These are designed to help you understand what you may be experiencing and how ACT can help you reclaim or, for some people, initially claim your life.

Although ACT stands for Acceptance and Commitment Therapy, a quick way to understand it is Accept, Choose, and Take Action. The chapters in part 2 provide different types of activities to help you with these skill sets. Some people prefer to start by identifying their values as a grounding source of motivation, while others benefit more from first learning how to understand and accept their current reality better. Choose the path and steps that are best for you.

A for Accept
    Chapter 3: Stepping Back from Your Thoughts
    Chapter 4: Accepting That the Unpleasant Is Unavoidable
C for Choose
    Chapter 5: Inhabiting the Here and Now
    Chapter 6: Understanding Yourself and Your Life in a New Way
T for Take Action
    Chapter 7: Clarifying What Matters to You
    Chapter 8: Acting and Behaving in Accordance with Your Values

An Overview of Depression and ACT

This book is divided into two parts. The first part is designed to provide an overview of depression and of Acceptance and Commitment Therapy (ACT). Part 1 will help you learn more about depression and introduce you to ACT treatment, which both personal accounts and research show to be very effective treatment. Chapter 1 will help you learn more about depression, including what it is, how it feels, how it can impact your day, and more. Chapter 2 explores ACT, an evidence-based and promising support to address and heal depression.

Part 2 provides opportunities to practice the six positive psychological skills identified in ACT. If you are working with a therapist or group using ACT, you may want to jump to part 2.

CHAPTER 1

Understanding Depression

Depression impacts lives in a wide variety of ways, some more recognizable than others. You likely picked up this book because you or someone you care about has been diagnosed with depression or is showing patterns that might be related to depression. Depression is a very common disorder experienced by over 120 million people worldwide. This means that there are numerous thoughts and opinions about it. Some of these are supported by research and promote healing, while others may provide misinformation that can interfere with recovery.

This chapter introduces you to diagnostic information about depression, the different ways it may manifest, symptoms, risk factors, and common misunderstandings.

Depression can be mild or severe in the ways it impacts lives. You may experience some uncomfortable emotions while reading the areas where depression is described in detail. You may also feel a sense of relief to have your experience described. Please keep in mind that depression is very treatable. The last section of this chapter is designed to help you explore options you can use during and beyond this workbook.

Can You Relate?

LIFE AS A SINGLE PARENT was exhausting, but Maria enjoyed the richness of raising her two young sons and working for a tax accountant. She had help from her parents who lived nearby. Although they were older, and had some health issues, their caring for her boys after school provided the support she most needed. Maria had her down moments, feeling sad that her ex-husband Julio left and that she was too busy to date. Yet she also loved her home and work life.

Then news stories about COVID-19 began breaking. Her life changed dramatically. Soon, she and her sons were working and schooling from home. They no longer spent time physically with her parents because of health risks. Maria felt overwhelmed and hopeless. It became harder to fix healthy meals, so they snacked more. She worked around the boy's school schedule, which meant she was either helping them with school or playing catch-up with work.

Her sons were unhappy and often bored. She found herself snapping at them, which caused her to feel ashamed. She would tell herself what a horrible mother she was, and that it was no wonder Julio had left. She soon found it difficult to make the kids attend classes. Her boss grew frustrated as she was late again and again.

Eventually, Maria found herself staying in bed much of the day. She would listen to her sons fight. She felt disgusted with herself and guilty, too. No matter how often she told herself to get up and take care of things the way she had, her body felt heavy and as if it were weighing her down. "What's wrong with me?" she asked herself again and again.

What Is Depression?

In day-to-day life, people often say they have depression when they feel down. The label "depressed" helps communicate that they feel sad enough to want support and maybe need a break from usual demands. Used this way, depression is an emotional state that invites support and adjustment to life's disappointments. Once the feelings have been experienced and shared, they tend to dissipate. Feeling down varies from person to person and time to time, but there are some commonalities to the experience as well.

Depression is also a shorthand term for the common but serious mood disorder diagnosed as Major Depressive Disorder (MDD). Clinical depression, a term indicating MDD symptoms meet diagnostic criteria, lasts at least two weeks and causes mild to severe symptoms that can affect how you feel, think, and handle daily activities. The World Health Organization reports that roughly 5 percent of people experience clinical depression. Left untreated, depression can result in reduced quality of life for the individual with depression and those connected to them. Additionally, clinical depression is a primary cause of suicide with nearly 46,000 Americans dying by suicide in 2020. We will dive deeper into clinical depression and the ways in which it manifests in peoples' lives.

The good news? Depression is very treatable, and you are not alone. Roughly 80 to 90 percent of people diagnosed with depression overcome the symptoms and create a satisfying life.

Common Symptoms

Depression has a wide variety of symptoms because it can affect many different systems within the mind and body. One person may keep very busy, while another may be unable to get out of bed. Someone who unintentionally loses weight at one stage of depression may unintentionally gain weight in another. However, there are common symptoms doctors have identified within the range of experiences.

The two hallmarks of depression, described in the next subsections, are feeling hopeless and losing interest in things that you typically find engaging. In clinical depression, these hallmarks are present most of the time for longer than two weeks. Additionally, depression impacts thoughts, feelings, behaviors, and bodily experience in a variety of ways. The chart that follows, though not exhaustive, lists some of the major symptoms of depression.

Ways Depression Can Impact Us

FEELINGS

Sorrow

Guilt

Shame

Hopeless

Helpless

Overwhelmed

Trapped

Unmotivated

Irritable, angry

THOUGHT PATTERNS

Negative

Repetitive

All or nothing

Unpleasant memories

Dire predictions

Comparison to others

Increased thoughts of death

Suicidal thoughts

Homicidal thoughts

Difficulty concentrating

Confusion

BEHAVIORS

Changes in eating

Changes in sleeping

Isolating

Procrastinating

Reduced self-care

Self-destructive behaviors
(substances, self-harm,
compulsive behaviors, etc.)

Suicidal planning, preparation,
and action

BODY

Heaviness

Tension

Headaches

Digestive issues

Slowed movements

Agitated movements

Fatigue

Feeling Sad, Empty, or Hopeless

The classic symptom of depression is feeling profound sadness. People who have experienced clinical depression describe the feeling as substantially different from normal sadness. One common description is that depression feels as though a heavy blanket were covering them and they were powerless to remove it. Others describe a dark bleakness, a sense of impending doom that extinguishes hope. Other people describe a sense of emptiness, of disconnection from self and others. These feelings may vary in intensity throughout a day or week or be experienced as a chronic undertone, present even when attending to activities of regular life.

Lower Interest and Motivation

The second defining characteristic of depression is the loss or reduction of interest in doing activities that are usually engaging. This can include a drop in libido or loss of interest in hobbies and recreational, professional, and social activities. The reduction in interest and motivation to engage may be associated with fatigue or a sense of overwhelm with life's responsibilities. Clients describe the sense that any task requires more energy than is possible to call forth. Many people isolate more because the effort to speak with others feels overwhelming and doomed to failure because they can't imagine anyone would understand their pain and struggles.

Sleep Issues

Depression can alter the architecture or patterns of your sleep cycle, typically reducing the amount of time you spend in the deeper stages of sleep. The loss of deep sleep time can make it difficult to sleep for more than a few hours at a time. Concerns about being sleep deprived can make it difficult to return to sleep, further reducing the amount of sleep. Alternately, people experiencing depression can sleep many hours longer than usual yet awaken fatigued because of the reduced amount of deep sleep. Sometimes people alternate between periods of insomnia and oversleeping during a depressive cycle.

Always Staying Busy

Another common symptom of depression is constant busyness, driven by the perception that one cannot slow down. Some people describe a sense of dread or terror when they begin to slow down and quickly rush to avoid that feeling with new activities. While busyness and a task-list focus may allow someone to avoid noticing their depression, it often creates exhaustion and interferes with mindful self-care, satisfying personal connections, and deep sleep. While family and friends can often recognize depression in people who lose interest and motivation, the busyness expression of depression is often misunderstood.

Feeling Overwhelmed and Irritable

Sadness is not always the dominant emotion in depression. Some people describe feeling "raw," easily irritated by things that usually do not disturb them. Clients describe feeling emotionally shaky, unable to understand their edginess or sense of being overwhelmed emotionally by minor events. Some people with depression may move quickly from irritation to rage, sometimes resulting in angry outbursts. In the context of depression, irritability and angry outbursts can lead to self-loathing and criticism, often creating a roller coaster of intense emotion. The anger also impacts relationships and can increase the isolation and lack of social support.

Where Does Depression Come From?

Despite significant research, the causes of depression have not been clearly identified. We have gained some key insights, such as identifying the neurotransmitter imbalances that occur when depression is present. Medications and lifestyle patterns that alter neurotransmitter levels are effective treatments. But do the imbalances cause depression? Or does depression cause the imbalances? We still don't know.

While direct causes have not been identified, risk factors have. For example, genetic research has identified over 269 genes and 102 variants that are associated with depression and can be defined as risk factors when present.

Challenging life experiences including traumatic events, significant loss, chronic neglect as a child, financial challenges, and medical or mental health diagnoses have been reported by individuals experiencing depression at higher rates than those without depression. The more such events or experiences an individual has, the greater likelihood that they may experience depression and that it may be more severe.

Self-defeating coping mechanisms form one of the risk factors that can be significantly impacted by psychotherapy. ACT identifies specific patterns that produce "psychological rigidity" and guides you in the development of psychological flexibility. You will learn more about these in chapter 2 and have the chance to develop these skills in the remaining chapters.

Inheritability

Depression can occur in families across generations, which raises the question of heritability. The transmission of depression within families appears to include both genetic and life patterning, or experiential, aspects. While no single gene or set of genes has been shown to definitively cause depression, parents and children may share an array of genes that creates susceptibility to depression.

Additionally, parents living with depression often model depressive thoughts, feelings, behaviors, and coping styles. When primary caregivers of young children are depressed, they tend to engage less frequently with them. Consequently, the children do not develop the secure emotional connection that can help prevent depression when life stressors occur.

Traumatic Life Events

Surviving a traumatic life event is a risk factor for the development of depression, as well as other mental health disorders. People who are assessed for lifetime trauma after receiving a major depression disorder diagnosis frequently report childhood abuse. Chronic, repetitive traumatic events as well as more separate traumatic events result in a higher risk for depression.

A review study showed 52 percent of people diagnosed with post-traumatic stress disorder (PTSD) also meet criteria for major depressive disorder (MDD). The two conditions share the following symptoms: difficulty concentrating, insomnia, change in appetite, loss of pleasure in activities, and irritability.

Other Mental Health Issues

Living with another mental health issue, particularly generalized anxiety and panic disorders, is a risk factor for depression. While studies show depression frequently occurs with mental health issues, including anxiety, stress disorders, OCD, schizophrenia, substance dependence, or eating disorders, depression usually starts after the other disorder. The more severe or difficult to treat the initial disorder is, the more likely depression is to develop.

The frequent co-occurrence of anxiety and depression has led to suggestions that they may share underlying processes. The National Institute for Mental Health developed the Research Domain Criteria (RDoC) to research "new ways of classifying mental disorders based on behavioral dimensions and neurobiological measures."

Self-Defeating Coping Mechanisms

Self-defeating coping mechanisms are patterns of thinking and behaving that block personal achievement. Some examples include procrastination, perfectionism, neglecting self-care, self-pity, blaming yourself or others, and using mood-altering substances to escape situations or feelings.

These are common human experiences that interfere with pursuing one's dreams if the person does not learn the tools to manage or prevent them. Left unchallenged, they can claim a larger percentage of someone's life and create a risk factor for depression. They can feed the cycle of hopelessness about being able to recover or live a satisfying life.

Medical Conditions

Some medical conditions can directly cause depressive symptoms. For example, thyroid conditions can reduce the amount of serotonin (the "feel good" hormone), cause fatigue or agitation, and cause significant weight changes. This combination mimics clinical depression, yet the underlying cause is the thyroid condition. A critical step in evaluating a client for clinical depression is having potential medical conditions evaluated by a medical practitioner.

Additionally, being diagnosed with and living with a medical condition or injury can require major changes in lifestyle and opportunities in personal and professional domains. Facing the profound losses that can accompany a medical condition is a risk factor for depression.

Financial Stressors

Financial stress of various types is linked with depression in adults (Guan et al., 2022). Lower household income, a reduction in income, high debt levels, and the subjective experience of financial strain are financial stressors that are risk factors for depression. Younger adults who experienced financial difficulties as children have an increased chance of depression as well.

Gut Microbiota

Your gut microbiota consists of the trillions of microorganisms, mostly bacteria, that live in your intestinal tract and are involved in functions essential to your health and well-being. A growing body of research supports a strong connection between gut biota and our mental health (Sanada et al., 2020). Major Depressive Disorder is shown to be associated with limited diversity of gut biota. In some treatment studies, participants who took probiotics had fewer symptoms than the participants who did not receive probiotics.

The Difference Between Depression and Sadness

A defining feature of depression can be feeling profound sadness, which encourages people to confuse the words and ideas. We've all experienced sadness, and it is natural to try to understand others from our own experience. However, regardless of what others may say, depression is much more complex and difficult to manage than sadness. Calling clinical depression "sadness" makes light of the suffering and life difficulties that depression causes and can make it more difficult to get the appropriate help.

Sadness is a healthy human emotion, part of the limbic wisdom system that helps us navigate life. Depression lasts longer than sadness and reduces our ability to enjoy life and function as we typically do. The following chart shows some of the primary differences.

FEELINGS, THOUGHTS, BEHAVIORS	SADNESS	DEPRESSION
Might feel sad and express sorrow through crying	Yes	Yes. Might also feel anxiety, guilt, anger, hopelessness
Might spend more time alone or want comfort from others more	Yes	Yes
Feels better after crying or being comforted	Yes	Less likely
Appetite and eating patterns stay the same	Yes or brief changes	May eat more or less, often causing weight loss or gain
Sleep patterns stay the same	Yes or brief changes	May have difficulty falling or staying asleep or sleep more than usual
Can participate in regular activities	Yes	Work, school, and relationships impacted
Body feels heavy, sluggish, or agitated	No	Yes
Thoughts about death, self-harm, or suicide	Not likely	Often

Common Myths and Misconceptions

Humans often create stories or narratives to explain challenging situations. The more these narratives are grounded in a thorough understanding of a situation, the more they help us problem solve effectively. Explanatory narratives that aren't grounded in fact-based understandings are considered myths or misconceptions. Because depression is one of the most common mental health conditions, there are many myths and misconceptions about it.

Unfortunately, these myths and misconceptions become part of the problem when they integrate themselves into the self-belief system of someone struggling with depression, and invite further self-blame and hopelessness. When family members, coworkers, and friends believe and reinforce these misconceptions, they can, even with the best intentions, make it more difficult for the person with depression to trust or want to confide in them. This can foster isolation and deepen the patterns that hold depression in place.

The good news is that there is solid evidence showing these beliefs to be inaccurate and unhelpful. Learning how to challenge these misbeliefs within yourself and, when you are ready, with others, can help free you from their grip. Here are some of the most common myths and misconceptions concerning depression that we continuously work to remove.

Only People with Poor Self-Discipline Get Depressed

Among the more debilitating symptoms of clinical depression are fatigue, cognitive confusion, and loss of motivation, all of which profoundly impact productivity. Someone who is typically well-organized and disciplined may struggle when depressed to complete tasks they would otherwise handle readily. This misconception confuses the symptoms of depression with the person experiencing them.

Illness of any kind is inconvenient for the person struggling and for those who depend upon them. Blaming the person struggling for the impact of the illness on their lives is counterproductive at best. It's important to learn to step away from this misconception to reduce its potential of feeding the depression.

Talking About Depression Will Just Make It Worse

People often avoid talking about their depression out of concern that it will deepen the depression. While it is true that talking about depression may bring your attention to it and make it seem worse in the moment, that same attention is the source of healing.

Talking about depression acknowledges it and is often the first step in reaching out for help. Just as the process of cleaning a closet involves bringing the items out of the closet, the first step in addressing depression is acknowledging it. Choosing someone who listens well and supports your treatment goals and desires will help more.

You Will Need Medication the Rest of Your Life

Clients often have very mixed feelings about taking medication to help manage their depression. One concern I frequently hear is that if they start taking medication, they will need to take it for the rest of their lives. While this concept was once medically accepted, newer treatment models integrate tapering off antidepressants once the depression severity is reduced.

Just as someone with a sports injury may require a brace regularly while the injury heals and then taper off to use it only during times of high demand on the injured joint, antidepressants can be used only when the symptoms make doing so beneficial.

Treatment Can Help

Learning about depression can feel overwhelming and discouraging, but it is an important part of the work moving forward with your life. Sometimes people find the acknowledgement of their experiences validating.

Remember that depression is very treatable, even when very severe and debilitating. Newer psychotherapies including ACT show high rates of success and are effective strategies in treating depression. In addition, new modalities such as Transcranial Magnetic Stimulation (TMS), neurofeedback, and ketamine treatment are transforming the lives of people who have lived with severe depression for decades.

Each individual experiencing depression has a unique history of risk factors and resources. Evaluating what treatments to try and which lifestyle changes will be most beneficial can be very challenging yet rewarding in the end. This book is here to help you explore the ACT tools for coming to terms with your life experiences, including depression, and creating a purposeful life based on your values.

Key Takeaways

While sadness is a core emotion that we all experience in response to loss or change, depression settles in for at least two weeks and affects almost every aspect of our being—from our emotions and body sensations to our thoughts and behaviors. Learning about depression helps people understand and manage their personal experiences with it.

- ✓ Clinical depression is a common mood disorder that ranges from mild to severe and presents in a variety of ways.

- ✓ We don't yet know what causes depression. Risk factors include both genetic patterns and life events. The severity of depression correlates to the number and severity of challenging life events.

- ✓ There is considerable misinformation about depression, and this inaccurate information can make overcoming depression even more difficult. Many organizations are working to help people understand depression better as part of fighting it.

- ✓ Depression is very treatable, more than ever before. New treatments, including ACT, are helping people overcome depression in ways that are changing how we understand depression.

CHAPTER 2

An Introduction to ACT

Although ACT is one of the newer psychotherapies, the fundamental tenet of mindfully facing what one wants to avoid as a path to health has been recognized in many cultures. Old adages such as "Get back on the horse" encourage facing the uncomfortable, while "Do the next right thing" speaks to choosing to live by your values, even when overwhelmed. ACT integrates theory, neuroscience, mindfulness, and valued living to help people move past suffering and into satisfying lives.

The purpose of this chapter is to introduce you to the ACT model and how it can help you move past depression toward living a purposeful life. You may already be working with ACT and consider it helpful enough that you want more practice, or you may be trying to see whether this approach might be right for you. This chapter introduces you to the tools and knowledge you will need as you work through this book.

Discovering ACT

CAROL FELL INTO A DEEP depression following the death of her husband, Rob. They met while serving in Iraq, and their love deepened through their tour and return to civilian life. As they were preparing to buy their first home, Rob began coughing and experiencing chest pain. Tests showed he had advanced lung cancer. Carol cared for him through the difficult protocols, but the cancer did not respond to treatment. Rob died within weeks of the diagnosis.

Carol was devastated. The dreams they shared felt empty without him, and she often thought of taking her life to join him. Her mind kept replaying the scene of her handing him the soda he wanted the day he died. Each time, she blamed herself. "If I hadn't done that," she told herself, "maybe we would have had more time." She felt she did not deserve a happy life because she had failed him as he was dying. She had been unable to takes steps forward for several years when she began ACT.

Carol wanted to live in ways that would make Rob proud. Recognizing that helped her accept that she had to face her grief. She attended an intensive grief workshop, making sure she would not be alone afterward in case she needed support. She went forward, finding and buying the home they had dreamed of and felt more connected to him as she did. For Carol, accepting his death, learning to observe but not believe the grief thoughts, and living her dream ended the depression.

The Origins of ACT

ACT was created in the mid-1990s by Steven C. Hayes, Kelly G. Wilson, and Kirk D. Strosahl to address many forms of human suffering. ACT is based on Relational Frame Theory (RFT), a psychological theory of language that focuses on how humans create links between concepts, words, and images. This ability to see relationships forms an essential building block of "higher cognition," or human ability to connect. For example, relating ice to cold allows ice to be used to cool something judged "too warm."

RFT observes that while the relational skills the human mind developed to solve problems in the physical world are effective in that realm, they often interfere with our ability to address psychological problems. For example, linking sadness with the judgment "bad" encourages us to avoid experiencing the emotion.

The developers of ACT realized a new approach was needed to help people overcome mental and emotional suffering, an approach that invited perspective into and freedom from the relational structures built into our language patterns. They combined mindful awareness of internal experiences with acceptance of those experiences and paired this mindful acceptance with values-based behavioral change techniques. ACT is considered part of the "third wave" of cognitive behavioral therapies because the focus is on how the person understands and relates to their thoughts and emotions, rather than on the content of them. Over time, the label "psychological flexibility" was added to describe the state of being present that allows people to thrive.

ACT can effectively treat a wide range of mental and emotional disorders because it's based on the human mental processes that lead to suffering and mental health challenges, rather than specific challenges. Early studies identified ACT as an effective treatment for depression as well as anxiety, PTSD, chronic pain, and other conditions.

The Intention of ACT

The fundamental goal of ACT is to help you live a more meaningful life by increasing your ability to live in the present moment, responding to both internal and external experiences. ACT is built around the idea that people suffer when they treat internal experiences such as thoughts, feelings, and sensations as something to be avoided or controlled. This suffering can take many forms, including depression, anxiety, and physical pain. ACT teaches people how to change their relationship with these internal experiences. When thoughts, emotions, and sensations are understood to be simply what they are—thoughts, emotions, and sensations—rather than as fundamental truths about one's identity and the broader world, they lose their power to limit people.

Unlike modalities like Cognitive Behavioral Therapy (CBT), which teach us how to challenge and reduce irrational thoughts or dysfunctional feelings that cause suffering, ACT acknowledges that suffering is a natural part of life. Instead of trying to change thoughts and feelings, ACT encourages changing your relationship with your experience. ACT uses metaphors and experiential exercises to help accept your feelings, thoughts, memories, and bodily sensations. This frees you to define your values and commit to live in ways that create a satisfying, rich life. As people begin to live in a values-based present, the suffering and symptoms that led them to therapy are replaced by positive, self-reinforcing psychological skills.

Acceptance

In ACT, acceptance is admitting to ourselves that the world, our lives, and our experiences are what they are, some delightful and others deeply painful. Accepting that abuse, war, illness, and injustice occur means they must be acknowledged, but not that they must be tolerated. Acceptance acknowledges that all our thoughts, feelings, and experiences are valid.

We accept the challenge to stay present to what is, rather than to avoid or deny it. Although it can seem counterintuitive, accepting that unwanted realities are part of life allows us to be present, centered, and less buffeted by difficult emotions, thoughts, and sensations.

Commitment

People with a sense of their purpose in life describe themselves as happier, more productive, and more present. ACT helps you commit to finding and living by your purpose. The steps help you identify your values in the various life domains—personal growth, relationships, work, etc.—and then define and commit to taking the actions that will move you forward.

Committing to take the actions that let you live a values-based life is not a promise to be perfect or a prediction of completing goals. Instead, it is a commitment to knowing your values and both defining and doing the actions that will help you live the life you most want.

Therapy

Therapy helps us face and change the patterns that interfere with living our lives fully and authentically. ACT is a structured approach shown to help people heal and create a more satisfying life. Although a book is not therapy in the original sense of the word defined by regular meetings with a therapist, the practices in this workbook can help you break free from some of the patterns of depression and learn to thrive.

Depression varies greatly in intensity and tenacity. What level of depression are you currently experiencing? What type of support, in addition to this book, might help you move from depression to living with more meaning and satisfaction?

ACT and Depression

ACT is a transdiagnostic approach, which means it was developed to address the conditions that underlie many mental health issues, instead of any specific disorder. Despite not being developed to treat depression, research shows ACT is an effective form of treatment for depression. If we think about risk factors for depression, it's clear that difficult life experiences in the absence of skills and resources to process those experiences play an important role. ACT is beneficial because it teaches us how to accept and come to terms with the unwanted life experiences, and to build a purposeful life based on personal values. Living with purpose, even in the presence of significant threat, allows us to live with vitality and commitment.

ACT's limitations include that it does not specifically address core issues, including traumatic events or childhood challenges. Additionally, evidence suggests that as a stand-alone treatment it is most effective with mild to moderate depression and that additional treatment options may be warranted for severe depression.

Psychological Flexibility

You may have heard athletes describe "being in the zone," the times they are fully present and able to respond to whatever the moment demands. For example, a cross-country skier in the zone can adjust rapidly to the contours of the slope, trees, rocks, rain, ice, and to the ways their body responds to the elements and physical demands.

Psychological flexibility occurs when we are in the zone in our day-to-day lives. It involves perceiving the many sources of information in the present moment—external and internal—while maintaining or changing behaviors to align with personal values. ACT teaches how to develop psychological flexibility through six core therapeutic processes: 1. being present; 2. acceptance, breaking the power of limiting thoughts; 3. broadening the understanding of self; 4. defining personal values; and 5. committing to live by those values.

The experience of depression can sap the energy and willingness to be present, to accept unwanted realities and experiences, or to know and live by one's purpose. Instead of living in the empowered zone of psychological flexibility, depression can create a zone of hopelessness and despair. ACT breaks through this quicksand and gets lives back on track with psychological flexibility.

The Acceptance and Action Questionnaire allows you to assess your current level of psychological flexibility and track changes as you use the workbook. You can find a link in the Resources section in the back of this book.

FEAR

Just as the opposite of physical flexibility is stiff or rigid muscles, the opposite of psychological flexibility is psychological rigidity. Psychological rigidity can develop and be maintained for a variety of reasons. While we need to recall the past and prepare for possible future events, the pattern of being distracted from the present by memories or future projections based on limited self-knowledge interferes with the ability to adapt. Avoiding uncomfortable internal experiences limits our self-knowledge, particularly around our values and the life we most want, and often leads to patterns of inaction and impulsivity. For example, someone avoiding the grief they feel over a lost loved one may stop doing activities that remind them of that person and the absence of that person in the present moment.

Another key factor is becoming attached to the stories we tell about ourselves, such as "I am a depressed person" or "I am bad at connecting with other people." While such familiar stories may bring temporary relief from facing unknown possibilities, they limit growth.

ACT defines the cause of many issues represented in the acronym FEAR. FEAR (Fusion, Evaluation, Avoidance, Remoteness) summarizes the internal processes that ACT identifies as the primary patterns blocking psychological flexibility, which we will break down next.

Fusion with Your Thoughts

Our thoughts often reduce complex, multifaceted ideas to simple statements that become part of our identity. For example, someone may say, "I am depressed," which fuses an emotion or condition with their identity. A more accurate description would be "I am a person currently experiencing the emotion or condition called depression." This statement acknowledges that a person is more than a given emotion and that the experience is not permanent.

The power of the idea "I am depressed" is like wearing sunglasses that dampen the beauty of the world and forgetting we are wearing them. Our identity can become fused with a thought and color our world.

Evaluation of Experience

Part of understanding our world is comparing things and evaluating them: higher vs lower, closer vs farther, better vs worse, and good vs bad are a few examples. Although this ability allows us to describe and transform the outer world, when we apply this pattern to our thoughts and feelings it can strengthen fusions. Feeling sorrow can be labeled "bad" and a person who experiences anger can be labeled "unhealthy." Smiling and expressing happiness, even if faked, may be labeled "good."

Such evaluations feed depressive patterns. Rather than considering evaluations as negative, ACT reduces the dominance of the evaluative words.

Avoidance of Your Experience

A fast way to "feel better" is to avoid an unpleasant thought, feeling, or experience. This instant reward reinforces avoidance. Although in the short term, avoidance might allow us to miss out on a painful experience, the long-term consequences can be detrimental.

For example, when we avoid going to the dentist, we escape the potential pain of a cavity being found and filled. Yet we are setting in place the possibility of more pain and anxiety if the cavity worsens due to our avoidance. Similarly, we may appreciate the short-term relief of avoiding sadness, anger, or anxiety, but we are opening the door to more distress.

Remoteness

When we are present, we often feel connected to both ourselves and the world. Depression and other patterns that break this connection can leave us feeling detached or more remote. We might feel as though we are watching life go by. Greens aren't as green, warm is not as warm, and natural beauty seems irrelevant.

Being distant or remote from ourselves can occur in many ways. We might feel disconnected from our body, our emotions, our important people, our history, events around us, our sense of meaning. Remoteness is one of the blocks to experiencing our lives directly.

The Core Therapeutic Processes of ACT

ACT's answer to the core problems identified in FEAR is to increase psychological flexibility, the ability to be present in the moment, and either change behaviors or continue them in alignment with personal values and commitments. The model defines six primary therapeutic processes that help free people from these thought patterns. The Mindfulness and Acceptance Therapeutic Processes include cognitive defusion, acceptance, and the observing self. The Commitment and Behavior Change Therapeutic Processes include contacting the present, defining valued directions, and committed action.

These areas are considered positive psychological skills that will help you live your life with purpose, able to navigate wanted and unwanted changes with conscious intention. Although the goal of ACT is to create a values-based, fulfilling life rather than to reduce the symptoms of depression or other mental health challenges, research shows that ACT is effective at reducing the symptoms of many disorders, including depression.

Part 2 of this workbook includes six chapters, one for each of the ACT therapeutic processes. The exercises, practices, and prompts in each chapter are chosen to help you develop the positive psychological skill for that particular process. Because the processes are interrelated and support each other, you can choose to do the activities in the order that feels most comfortable to you.

Cognitive Defusion

Our minds constantly generate thoughts, which may evoke emotions, sensory experiences, and a drive to behave in a certain way. The natural tendency is to consider these thoughts to be literally true and to express truths about our identity and even the world outside ourselves. ACT defines this as cognitive fusion.

Defusion or de-fusion is an invented word to describe the process of learning to separate from our thoughts and emotions. ACT provides many tools for learning how to break the fusion, including witnessing the flow of thoughts, repeating words at varying frequencies and tones, and describing or changing characteristics of the thought.

Acceptance

Acceptance of internal events such as thoughts and emotions is a powerful alternative to avoiding them. Acceptance of feelings frequently experienced by people diagnosed with depression, such as sorrow and anger, involves full recognition of the experience and that these emotions are a natural part of life. They do not need to be criticized or changed.

In ACT, acceptance of emotions is not an end itself. Feelings provide insight into our values and the ways our values are not being upheld. For example, we may feel deep sorrow because we feel disrespected in a relationship and don't know how to address it.

Contacting the Present

ACT encourages being present in the moment, aware of and responding to the environment and internal experiences without judgment. Awareness acknowledges ongoing details such as those in a near car accident—the presence of sunlight reflecting on the hood, hand raised to block the glare, the ability to see a car too close for safety, the need to brake rapidly, the feel of the car slowing down, perhaps tires screeching, the sense of relief with the heart still pounding rapidly, lightly touching hands with a passenger and relief laughter inviting deeper breaths. Often a scary experience such as the one described brings us more fully to the present. Being fully present in the moment frees us to respond fully and appropriately to the current, ever-changing demands.

Three Forms of Self

ACT defines three forms of self. The conceptualized-self is our identity based on our lives and experiences of ourselves in the world, our unfiltered self-perceptions. Some aspects of the conceptualized-self include factual aspects such as where we are born and our height. However, the conceptualized-self is often defined by fusions and judgments. For example, our conceptualized-self might define us as unlovable or as unable to have a satisfying life.

Fortunately, we are much more than our conceptualized-self. ACT defines the observing-self as the part of ourselves that notices our thoughts, feelings, and other aspects of how we experience the world. During ACT, you will learn to strengthen your observing-self. This helps invite you to live more in the present and to defuse from your internal experiences.

The third sense of self that ACT defines is the self-as-context, the self that is present to the flow of your experiences and allows you to make choices in the moment. We experience psychological flexibility when we are living from the self-as-context, aided by the observing-self. In essence, the self-as-context is built on the idea that humans are not the content of their thoughts or feelings, but rather the consciousness experiencing those thoughts and feelings.

Values

People experiencing depression often say their life has no meaning or purpose. ACT invites people to identify the values that underlie their life's purpose. ACT defines values as the deeply held principles of living that serve as an individual's true north. Values are action-oriented and may vary across the different domains of a life.

For example, one person may define the values of being a fair and motivating manager at work, a loving and responsible parent, and a skilled artist who experiences personal transformation through their creativity. ACT guides the exploration of personally chosen values in the relevant domains for each person.

Committed Action

ACT's ultimate goal is to help people live a purposeful life filled with values-based actions. While values define someone's guiding direction, committed action involves naming and committing to the short- and long-term tasks and goals that express those values.

For example, someone whose depression began after a car crash injured their back and made walking painful might have chosen the values of promoting their physical and mental health throughout their lives and contributing to charitable causes. Committed action might include starting work with a physical therapist and exploring new ways of being physically active that can eventually raise money for charities. You will have the chance to choose the values and commit to the actions that will be most meaningful to you.

Key Takeaways

ACT is a psychotherapy that focuses on the underlying patterns that cause human suffering rather than a specific diagnosis. It is considered part of the third wave of cognitive behavioral therapies because it focuses on how a person relates to internal experiences of thoughts, urges, and sensations rather than the content of those thoughts and internal experiences.

✓ Instead of focusing on addressing symptoms, ACT helps people develop positive psychological skills including being in the present and identifying personal values.

✓ The acronym FEAR (Fusion, Evaluation, Avoidance, Remoteness) summarizes the primary patterns blocking psychological flexibility.

✓ The core processes for moving from psychological rigidity to flexibility are: cognitive defusion, acceptance, and allowing the observing self to help you step away from a self that is defined by your life experiences toward one able to respond in the moment.

✓ The core processes for creating a purposeful life are: being in the present moment, identifying values, and committing to making life changes based on those values.

✓ Research shows ACT is an effective treatment for depression.

PART II

Building an ACT Practice for Depression

As we move into part 2 of the workbook, you will find information, exercises, prompts, and activities to help build your personal ACT practice for moving beyond depression. Part 2 is divided into six chapters, one for each of the core ACT processes. The following chart gives you space to make notes as you work through the chapters. You may want to identify activities you found helpful, write down questions, or keep track of dates you work on a chapter.

CHAPTER	TITLE	NOTES
3	Stepping Back from Your Thoughts	
4	Accepting That the Unpleasant Is Unavoidable	
5	Inhabiting the Here and Now	
6	Understanding Yourself and Your Life in a New Way	
7	Clarifying What Matters	
8	Acting and Behaving in Accordance with Your Values	

CHAPTER 3

Stepping Back from Your Thoughts

We spend much of our awake time thinking, with estimates that the average person has between 6,000 to 70,000 thoughts per day! Research suggests that the majority of these thoughts are negative. Why? Because our brains are trained to survive, and survival means problem-solving. Our brains excel at finding problems to address, and that means noticing the negative.

Until we examine them, thoughts and even words are fused with emotions, sensory information, body sensations, and prior experiences. For example, someone who had a near-drowning experience as a child in a lake may not remember the experience consciously but might feel anxious and down when they see a lake or hear the word "lake." The various components of the memory—thoughts, feelings, body sensations, and behavioral urges—all fuse together.

The activities in this chapter will help you notice the experience of fusion, from the simple level of understanding a word like "orange" to the more complex fusions created during challenging life experiences. You will learn how to separate yourself from the thoughts and other internal experiences that help hold your depression in place. One classic ACT metaphor is learning to see thoughts as clouds in the sky and allowing them to drift away in the wind. Another tool is to label thoughts as something our minds generate rather than believing each thought.

Living Single

DESPITE STEADY PROMOTIONS AT HER dream job and solid friendships, Dinorah found herself despairing about ever finding a partner. Her long-term partner, Elsa, whom she'd wanted to marry and raise children with, had cheated on her and left her for someone else right before the COVID-19 pandemic started. The social isolation limited her chances at meeting new people, and she told herself she was doomed to live her life alone.

Overall, Dinorah was gregarious and confident with no difficulty meeting new people for work or friendship. When it came to dating though, she froze and told herself no one would ever want her. She would start to flirt, but then the belief that no one would find her attractive silenced her.

Dinorah was in fact creating distance from a painful narrative in her own life. In middle school, Dinorah's friends knew she had a crush on a girl named Abby and told her that Abby had similar feelings. Based on their encouragement, Dinorah asked Abby out, only to be told "No way, I don't even like you." Set up by her alleged friends, Dinorah lost confidence in her ability to tell whether someone liked her and lost trust in her friendships.

Labeling her dating anxiety as a thought she had because of her middle school experience helped Dinorah initiate conversations with women. At first, she felt socially awkward attempting these exchanges, but soon had more enjoyable conversations with the potential to be something more.

Learning How to Recognize Cognitive Fusion

Have you ever said or heard someone say, "I feel stuck in my head, separate from the rest of the world"? Those words describe cognitive fusion well—when we are so close to our thoughts that we believe them completely and cannot recognize that we are separate from our thoughts.

More Than Words

Words have the power to evoke feelings, body sensations, thoughts, and memories. This prompt invites you to experience that. Notice what you are feeling as you begin this writing exercise. Observe and jot down notes about your emotions and body sensations.

_____

_____

Now think about a favorite food or item from childhood. Name and describe it in detail. What color(s) was it? How did it smell? What was the texture? What makes it your favorite? Was this a private or shared treasure? How old were you when it was important to you? Let yourself connect with your favorite food or item, as though it were right in front of you.

_____

_____

_____

_____

Notice what you feel now, after writing about your childhood favorite item or food. Have your feelings or body experience changed?

_____

_____

_____

Let Your Mind Chatter

We become so used to our thoughts telling us things that we either don't notice our thoughts at all or notice them constantly. We may believe them without much review. This exercise will help you bring these thoughts out into the open. One way to think about it is our thoughts get stuck in patterns and "clog the drain." Allowing yourself to observe the thoughts can "unclog" them.

Choose a video clip with a main character from a source you like—movie, series, YouTube, TikTok, etc. Your role is to say out loud whatever thoughts come to mind as you observe the main character.

Refer to the main character as "you" and speak your thoughts that are relevant to the character as well as those that may not be. Anything goes. Include random observations like, "That door is so green it hurts my eyes," or "I don't know why you think going through that door is a good idea. You know there is trouble on the other side."

Understanding Your Thoughts in a New Way

Thoughts are typically linked to memories, emotions, body sensations, and urges. This exercise helps you understand and work with the associations a given thought has for you. This is one way to defuse from a troubling thought.

First, identify a troubling thought. Something like "I don't want anyone to see me today. I better stay home." Write it here.

_____

Next, answer some questions about it.

What feelings, if any, are linked to this thought?

_____

_____

_____

_____

What body sensations, if any, are linked to this thought?

_____

_____

_____

_____

What do you typically do when you have this thought?

_____

_____

_____

_____

Write the thought in the center circle of the following image.

The next step is to explore perceptions you might have about the thought. If it had a color, what color would it be? Write the color in the image that follows. Then complete the other descriptors in the image for this thought.

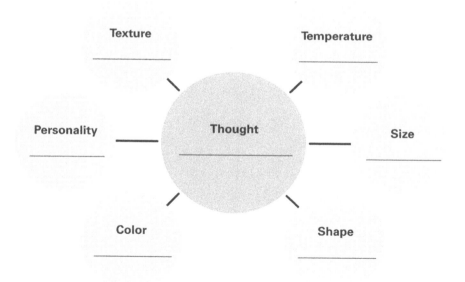

Give the thought a nickname on the line provided and draw it on the next page.

Nickname: _____

What do you now notice about the thought? Has it changed as you spend time with it? How has your relationship to the thought changed?

_____

_____

Thought patterns are often habit-based. What will you notice about this thought when your mind thinks it again?

_____

_____

Learning How to Defuse Your Thoughts

Sound Play

Words have the power to change our mood, our state of being, energy level, and much more. Think of a word or phrase that brings you down. Examples include: "depressed," "worthless," "failure," "hopeless," or "loss." Are there any changes that occur in your body as you think about your word or phrase? How does your neck feel? Your chest? Does tension develop in your body as you think about this word? This practice is designed to help break the fusion between the word and how that word affects you.

Try some or all of the following:

- Say the word ten times quickly. Change the pitch and rhythm as you repeat the word another ten times.

- Repeat the word eight times in a deep voice, then eight more times in a silly voice.

- Hum the word to three different rhythms—somber, marching band, festive, children's song.

- Change the first letter to match the alphabet—"depressed" might become "apressed," "bepressed," "cepressed," and so forth all the way to "zepressed." Notice any versions that you like.

After you have done the exercises you chose, take a moment to check in with yourself. How does your body feel now? Say the word in a normal tone. How does the word affect you now?

Remote Control

One way to gain perspective on negative self-beliefs is to imagine them outside ourselves and then alter the image. On the TV screen shown here, write down a negative self-belief, such as "I am a loser" or "It is all my fault."

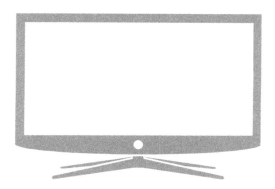

How true does it feel?

1. Close your eyes and imagine you have a remote control that can move and alter the negative thought you wrote down. You can hold your actual TV remote if it helps.

2. Using your hand, have the remote move the thought around the screen. Change the speed. If your mind resists trying this or other parts of the activity, tell your mind, "Thank you for resisting, Mind, but I am going to do this anyway. You can help me evaluate whether it helped after we do this."

3. Use the remote to change the color of the thought: red, orange, yellow, green, blue, purple. What colors soften the thought?

4. Shrink the thought, then expand it, and shrink it again. Put the thought in a container and use the remote to hold it there. Let it come out. What does it do now?

5. Create animation effects for your thought. Does it sparkle? Evaporate? Turn inside out?

Now how true does the thought feel?

1	2	3	4	5	6	7	8	9	10
False			Somewhat True				True		

How did it feel to have the thought outside of you and responding to your wishes? Check back with your mind to evaluate the results.

_____

_____

_____

_____

_____

_____

_____

_____

_____

_____

_____

_____

Help Your Negative Judgments Swim Away

Finding ways to involve your body in releasing negative thoughts can broaden the experience. For this exercise you will need small sticky notes.

1. In the following picture, color the human image to represent yourself. Add clothes, hair, and any details that allow you to recognize it as you.

2. Color the water in the stream. Allow yourself to have a sense of the water flowing from left to right. If it helps, put on some ambient noise of a stream or wooded scene. As you work, imagine yourself sitting by the stream and allow your thoughts to flow.

3. As thoughts enter your mind, write each thought on a separate sticky note until you have collected six to eight. It's okay if the same thought keeps reoccurring. Write it down on a different sticky note each time it does.

4. Now take the first thought and place the sticky note on the first text box fish.

5. Take a deep breath, then move the note one box to the right.

6. Add the next thought to the leftmost box. Notice that these are your thoughts and that you are separate from your thoughts.

7. Continue this process, allowing each thought to be moved to the right one box at a time.

8. When a thought reaches the rightmost box, move it away from the drawing. Notice what it feels like to watch as your thoughts move away from you. These are your thoughts, and you can let them be just thoughts.

When to Use Defusion

How do you know when to try a defusion technique like Remote Control (page 39) or Sound Play (page 38)? We often get caught up in fused patterns. Here are some indicators to help you determine when to use your defusion techniques:

- You notice you are making many comparisons and evaluations.
- You are mentally somewhere else.
- Your mind feels busy or confused.
- Your thoughts feel old, tired, too familiar.

How do you know if the technique worked?

- Can you see the thought as a thought rather than as a truth now?
- Does the thought seem less believable now?
- Do you feel less distress?

This table provides space for you to make notes on which defusion techniques you found helpful or unhelpful.

DEFUSION TOOL	WHEN/WHY YOU TRIED IT	HOW WELL IT WORKED
Sound Play		
Remote Control		
Help Your Negative Judgments Swim Away		

CONTINUED

When to Use Defusion   CONTINUED

DEFUSION TOOL	WHEN/WHY YOU TRIED IT	HOW WELL IT WORKED
Labeling Thoughts, Sensations, Emotions, and Behaviors		
Word Swap		

Your Relationship to Your Thoughts

Humans are complex beings with thoughts, emotions, body sensations, behavioral urges, and choices, all of which build habits through our life experiences. Much of our sense of identity is based on our thoughts, which gives those thoughts great power, especially when we don't notice them. You may have experienced a change of opinion after talking with someone or journaling—processes that invite us to become aware of our thoughts. ACT invites greater personal freedom and choice by changing the relationship to our thoughts.

Journal about your relationship with your thoughts, including how the relationship varies. Do you believe and act upon your thoughts without noticing? What happens when you have thoughts that contradict each other? Which thoughts do you feel are more "you"?

_____

_____

_____

_____

_____

_____

_____

_____

_____

_____

_____

Disobey Your Thoughts

You can do this practice with someone you know or using a recorded workout or exercise program. The goal is to become more comfortable acting independently from your thoughts.

- If you are working with a partner, have them do an action such as touching their nose with their thumb. Say out loud, "I must touch my nose with my thumb" while doing a different action such as swinging your arms.

- If you are watching an exercise or workout recording, choose one of the actions the instructor directs such as doing a sit-up. Say out loud "I must do a sit-up" while doing a different action such as sitting down and picking up a book.

- Repeat this process for at least ten different actions.

If you are working with a partner, switch roles and let them have a chance to perform the activity. Then talk with each other about how it felt to disregard your thoughts and take different actions.

Reflecting on the Experience

How might this activity apply to disregarding thoughts linked to depression?
Why is it important to be able to disregard directions from your thoughts at times?
Journal about how it felt.

_____

_____

_____

_____

_____

_____

_____

_____

_____

_____

_____

_____

Labeling Thoughts, Sensations, Emotions, and Behaviors

One classic way to create distance between the fusion that can occur between your thoughts and identity is to acknowledge that it is your mind that is thinking the thought. When you think, "I don't enjoy myself when I have free time," acknowledge the thought as, "My mind is thinking that I don't enjoy myself when I have free time."

Try this with a few of your own painful thoughts.

Thought: _____

My mind is thinking . . . _____

_____

_____

Thought: _____

_____

My mind is thinking . . . _____

_____

Given how deeply interwoven our thoughts are with emotions, body sensations, urges, and behaviors, you can add to the defusion process by acknowledging the connection.

Let's revisit the free time example and change it to include how our entire being is affected: "When my mind thinks that I don't enjoy myself during free time, my chest tightens and my stomach drops. Then my mind thinks that I am hopeless and will never be happy."

Complete some of the patterns you experience in the following table. The first row has an example.

WHEN MY MIND THINKS . . .	MY [BODY PART]	MY EMOTIONS	I HAVE THE URGE TO . . .
That I'm stupid and will never get my taxes done	*My stomach feels nauseous*	*And my confidence drops, leaving me scared*	*Call in sick*

Defusing from Depressing Thoughts

Depressing thoughts tend to be negative and, to the extent we believe them or are fused with them, bring us down. Examples include thoughts such as "I hate my life," 'I'll always be alone," or "Nothing ever gets better." This subsection will help you identify and learn to defuse from depressive thought patterns.

Word Swap

We all become entangled in our thoughts and personal narratives. The more we tell our stories, the more likely we are to believe them and live our lives accordingly. Words like "depressed" bring up many associations such as "heavy," "alone," "burden," "hopeless." Complete the following exercise to learn how to weaken the associations you have with moods.

Complete the following sentences.

When I get **depressed**, I _____

_____ .

On my **worst** days, I _____

_____ .

Hopelessness feels like _____

_____ .

If _____

had never happened, I would be _____

_____ .

When my body feels **heavy**, I know that _____

_____ .

Nobody understands/cares [what I've been through/how it affects me . . .]

_____ .

After writing your responses, what do you notice about your mood and energy?

Now complete the sentences again, this time replacing the words in bold with a category of words such as fruits or mailing items. You can ask a friend to provide words or use a word generator. The first one is done to provide an example.

When I get [**apple**], I _____ .

On my _____ days, I _____

_____ .

_____ feels like _____

_____ .

If _____ had never

happened, I would be _____ .

_____

When my body feels _____ , I know

that _____ . _____ understands/

cares [what I've been through/how it affects me] _____ .

How does it feel to have the associations broken? Word swapping helps us see how many concepts and internal experiences we have fused with certain words or experiences.

Labeling "Sticky" Thoughts

"Sticky" thoughts are the ones that seem to hold on no matter how hard we try to ignore them or get rid of them. They often resist efforts at defusion and keep repeating insistently in ways that make it difficult to be present. While sometimes they can be intrusive, they can also be the ones we "know better" than to believe so they escape our notice. Journaling can help us notice them and defuse from them.

1. Choose a distressing situation you face, one that is the right level for you in this moment.

2. Set a timer for twenty minutes and journal about this situation. When you hear the timer, stop writing. Thank yourself for putting your thoughts and feelings down. Take a stretch break.

3. When you are ready, read what you wrote from the perspective of a good friend. Notice and label thoughts using the following.

   a. List three descriptive thoughts.

   b. List three evaluative or judgmental thoughts.

   c. List and label thoughts as memory, image, blame statement, should statement, question. Which invite distress?

   d. Name three difficult thoughts.

Depression Myths

There are many false beliefs about depression that feed its power. What myths about depression have impacted you? Write about choices you made and make in your life based on these common myths and add any others you feel you need to acknowledge. Some examples are provided.

DEPRESSION MYTH	SHORT-TERM IMPACTS	LONG-TERM IMPACTS
Depression is always passed on from parent to child		Deciding not to have children to avoid passing on the illness
Only lazy people get depression	Hide the depression from loved ones	
Talking about depression makes it worse		
Antidepressants are the only effective treatment for depression		

Wounded Thought Patterns

Research shows that writing about painful life experiences can reduce emotional distress and reveal the limiting beliefs that often develop in response to them. Choose an aspect of your life that you feel depressed about. It may be a one-time event such as an accident or trauma, or a chronic situation such as an illness that affects you or a loved one, or a harmful behavior. Find a time and place to write where you won't be interrupted for twenty to thirty minutes. Set a timer and write whatever comes up.

_____

_____

_____

_____

_____

_____

_____

_____

_____

Now review what you wrote and highlight or circle any statements that define you in a limited way such as "I am traumatized for life" or '"I am broken." The thoughts or beliefs that develop around a painful experience are often the ones we are most fused with. Choose one that showed up in your writing to practice a defusion technique with.

The Non-Depressed You

Memories tend to follow moods. When we are sad, we recall sad memories; when anxious, anxious memories; and when content, memories of being content. This pattern, called state-dependent memory, can make it difficult to remember times we were not depressed.

Write about who you are when you are not experiencing depression. What do you enjoy? What moments are special to you? What characteristics do you appreciate about yourself? If you feel stuck, ask someone who knows you to help you remember or look at photos or videos of a happy time.

_____

_____

_____

_____

_____

_____

_____

_____

_____

_____

Spheres of Connection

We tend to thrive when we have frequent, safe connections that range from deeply intimate to casual. Depression and losses can weaken our connections and make it more difficult to form new ones. This exercise will help you see both where you have connections and identify places to form new ones or deepen existing ones.

1. Draw a circle, roughly an inch wide. Write your name in it.

2. Draw three more circles around the first circle creating a "bullseye" image. These circles represent how close you feel to the people in your life.

3. In the second circle, write the name of anyone you trust or can depend on.

4. In the third circle, write the names of people who are part of your life in a regular way that aren't part of your inner circle.

5. In the fourth circle, add those you encounter in more casual ways: grocery clerks, coworkers, etc.

6. If there are people you have lost to death, disagreement, or other reasons, you may want to include their names to acknowledge the loss. Add them in the circle where they belonged before you lost them or where you miss them now.

7. How does it feel to see your relationships and the potential need for more and stronger ones? How might you begin to fill out the circles to enrich your life?

Build Your Support Network

Most people are harsher on themselves than they are on everyone else, but establishing a support system can help break some of those fusions that hold your depression in place. In this practice, you will identify people who help you break free from negative thoughts, even if only sometimes, and ways to ask for their support as you tackle your depression in new ways. If there isn't anyone now, you can begin steps to finding someone. The following chart lists several examples to help you get started.

CATEGORY/NAME	STATUS	STEP TO TAKE
Family member/Sade	*Sister reminds me of my strengths and that I'm not always depressed*	*Ask her to do exercises with me*
Coworker/Jim	*Helps me see the bigger picture with work stressors, that most aren't my fault*	*Spend more time with him; invite him to lunch*
Therapist/Dante	*Understands me, cares, listens*	*Share this book with them, ask them to do exercises with me*

CONTINUED

Build Your Support Network   CONTINUED

CATEGORY/NAME	STATUS	STEP TO TAKE
Support group	*Don't have one, can't afford one*	*Pick a free support program listed in the back of this book and contact your local branch*

Developing Self-Compassion

Self-compassion is another powerful way to break cognitive fusions, in part because depressive thoughts are often self-critical and blaming. Compassion offers kindness in the presence of pain or suffering. Write down some people, either in your life or famous individuals, who express compassion in ways you can feel. Animals are often solid sources of love and compassion, so feel free to include them.

_____

_____

_____

_____

What do you feel as you think about the people or animals you listed?

_____

_____

_____

Think of a time when you experienced someone showing you compassion. What did it feel like?

_____

_____

_____

What, if anything, changed for you? Describe it.

_____

_____

_____

If you can't recall anyone being compassionate to you, write about a time you witnessed someone being compassionate to someone else or a time you felt compassionate to someone.

_____

_____

_____

Describe a time in your life when you experienced suffering. If you are new to self-compassion, it is usually better to start with a small event and one that is easy to feel compassion about. Some people start with themselves as a child, dropping an ice cream cone or losing a game.

_____

_____

_____

Invite kindness and caring for yourself around this experience of suffering. What can you say to yourself to express the caring and compassion you feel?

_____

_____

Key Takeaways

Cognitive defusion is one of the six core therapeutic processes in ACT. Fusion refers to the ways our words and thoughts become linked to judgments, feelings, body sensations, behaviors, and memories. This chapter has provided various tools to help you identify and break the fusion patterns you have with words and thoughts.

- ✓ Cognitive fusion—the associations of given words and sentences with evaluations, emotions, and behaviors—causes automatic responses and reduces psychological flexibility.

- ✓ Learning to recognize and break through cognitive fusions is called cognitive defusion.

- ✓ Learning to identify the emotions, body sensations, and behavioral urges fused with a thought helps break the connections and allows you to see the thought as separate from yourself.

CHAPTER 4

Accepting That the Unpleasant Is Unavoidable

In this chapter we discuss the ACT process of acceptance. Acceptance means an active and conscious embrace of thoughts and feelings without attempting to avoid, stop, or lessen them. When we can't accept challenging events or internal experiences, we remain caught up in fighting or denying them. It is important to understand that accepting something is true does not mean we agree or condone it. As we accept uncomfortable experiences, thoughts, and emotions, we free ourselves from the struggle with them.

Navigating Withdrawal

CASEY WAS A MASTER AT emotional avoidance, focusing his energy on competency under stress. As a helicopter medic, he quickly took charge in rapidly evolving, life-threatening situations. Casey was deeply respected for his calmness and ability to evaluate risks and lead the team in ways that saved lives while anticipating and managing emergent hazards. Although memories of cumulative losses through the years sometimes kept him up at night, overall, his approach worked well. He enjoyed his work and his family life, and looked forward to the birth of his first grandchild.

After a car crash with a fatality, where he had managed to follow protocols and get the other parties to hospitals, he stopped eating for several days and withdrew into his workshop. He refused to see his children, particularly his pregnant daughter. His wife, boss, and colleagues were concerned and asked how to help. His behavior on the job changed, and he was put on medical leave until he could return with a clinician's note saying he was again fit for duty. Reluctantly, he sought treatment.

Building trust and a willingness to talk about any of the tragic events he had witnessed took months of weekly sessions. At times, he would quit therapy and then return after a few weeks. As he built his ability to accept the depth of pain and loss, sadness, and anger he felt, he became more willing to talk about the events of that day.

As he described approaching the driver's side and slowly taking in the evidence that a young pregnant woman was trapped with injuries so severe she would not likely survive removal, he began to sob. As Casey allowed himself to experience his grief over their deaths and his powerlessness to save them, he let go of the belief that he was a failure. Eventually, Casey was able to reconnect with his children and return to work.

Acceptance?

What does acceptance mean to you? In ACT, acceptance means that you can be present with your psychological experiences without moving into defensive behaviors. For example, someone who avoids sadness by drinking or self-harming would learn to accept the sadness as part of the human experience and choose not to drink or self-harm to avoid the sadness. In this subsection, you will learn more about how to accept your life and experiences.

I Will Never Accept

Being encouraged to accept unwanted experiences and realities often brings up strong resistance. Welcome your resistance. What will you never accept? What experiences in your life are completely unacceptable? What is intolerable about your life or the lives of others? Allow your feelings to flow as you write. What needs to change for life to be bearable? What should never have happened? Answer these questions on the following lines.

_____

_____

_____

When you are done, take a breath. What do you feel now? You may have touched anger or rage. Anger lets us know when boundaries have been violated and often points to deeper values. What values underlie your unwillingness to accept certain things?

_____

_____

_____

What Acceptance Is and Isn't

Acceptance acknowledges what is, without condoning or excusing it. Accepting that bad things happen and that people suffer as a result is acknowledging that this "thing" is true, whether or not we think it should be.

One way to understand the difference is to break down the attributes of something into primary attributes (facts) and secondary attributes (opinions). Acceptance means accepting that the primary attributes are true and that the secondary attributes are thoughts and feelings about the primary attributes.

Let's try an example.

1. Choose a mug or cup.

2. Describe it in terms of primary attributes: it's shape, color, size, heft.

3. Now describe your opinion of it: Is it attractive? Do you like the way it feels in your hands? Is it comfortable to drink from? These are secondary attributes, important to your experience but separate from the mug itself.

Acceptance means acknowledging that the size, color, shape, and other primary attributes are what they are. Acceptance also includes accepting your judgments about its appearance as secondary attributes—your judgment or opinions rather than facts. Our opinions matter, yet they are only opinions.

This is easier done with a mug than with our experiences, but both have primary and secondary attributes. Think about a distressing reality in your life and write about it for ten to fifteen minutes. Go back and mark primary versus secondary attributes. For example, the primary attributes about a job loss might include how long you have been out of work and how the job was lost, such as being let go because of a larger layoff or fired. Secondary attributes might include thoughts and feelings about the experience, yourself, and the world in reaction to the job loss.

Willingness

My clients often tell me that while sometimes they can do things they know help, other times they feel unwilling or unable to. Feeling miserable and unwilling to try something feels even more miserable, yet this fluctuation in willingness is a normal part of being human.

Journal about your experiences with being willing to take care of yourself, to try new things, to feel unwanted emotions. What invites willingness for you? What creates blocks? What different feelings do you have when you have strong resistance to doing something you "know" is "good for you"?

_____

_____

_____

_____

_____

_____

_____

_____

_____

_____

Accepting Your Life

Most of us have aspects of our lives that we deeply wish were not true and find difficult to accept. In this subsection, you will have the chance to name and begin to accept that, no matter how unwanted these experiences are, they happened and are part of your life history.

Name Your Losses

You likely noticed that many of the risk factors for depression are challenging life experiences and that the more such experiences a person has, the more likely they are to have depression and for the severity to be greater. This information can be discouraging because we can't change the fact that our life includes deep and often tragic loss.

While the events don't cause depression, they are usually difficult to accept, evoke unwanted and intense feelings, and invite limiting thoughts. The goal of this exercise is to help you identify the events and realities in your life that are most difficult to accept. If you need more room to include all the events, add extra pages or, if you prefer, write it electronically.

Going through the list may bring up painful memories and emotions. Allow yourself time for self-appreciation and gentle self-care after you complete it.

EVENT	HAPPENED TO ME Y/N?	AGE/ FREQUENCY/ DURATIONS	HAPPENED TO AN IMPORTANT PERSON Y/N?	AGE/ FREQUENCY/ DURATION
Medical illness				
Mental health challenge				

EVENT	HAPPENED TO ME Y/N?	AGE/ FREQUENCY/ DURATIONS	HAPPENED TO AN IMPORTANT PERSON Y/N?	AGE/ FREQUENCY/ DURATION
Neglect				
Change of community				
Job loss, financial challenges				
Loss of significant person for reason other than death				
Death of personally important individual				
Violence, abuse				
Natural disaster				
Other loss or difficult experience				
Unwanted sexual experience				
War/organized violence				

Take a few minutes to let in the reality that these experiences are part of your life. Which are the most difficult to accept? Which do you already accept?

Acknowledging Death

Death, our own and those of others, is one of the most difficult realities to accept. Western culture tends to deny death and actively seeks to extend life under most circumstances, which makes accepting death more challenging. Traditionally people of different generations shared living space and people died at home. This approach allows the natural order of death to be experienced and shared throughout life. Most of us haven't had that opportunity and so death seems more removed from life.

What are your thoughts and feelings about death? Your own death? The death of others? What familial, cultural, or spiritual values contribute to your experience of death now? What experiences have you had with loss through death? Include animals if you have loved and lost one or more.

_____

_____

_____

_____

_____

_____

_____

_____

_____

_____

Acknowledging Your Life

Few lives follow the script society prescribes for happiness—safe enriching childhood with two loving parents and caring siblings, extended family, health, success with academics, career, and friendships, loving partner and possibly children followed by grandchildren. The places where our lives diverge from this script often involve loss and pain. You may have a different script of what allows for a life of happiness, but there may still be places where your life went "off track."

In this exercise you create a timeline of the aspects of your life that met your script for a happy life and those that did not. The Name Your Losses activity (page 68) provides examples of experiences that alter lives profoundly. On the timeline that follows, write in the turning points of your life, the ones where your life went off the course you wanted it to take. What changed in your life as a result of these experiences?

HAPPY MOMENTS		
BIRTH		PRESENT

HARD MOMENTS		
BIRTH		PRESENT

Accepting Your Strengths

Accepting ourselves and our lives is more than facing the difficult aspects. Accepting ourselves includes embracing our strengths and the enjoyable aspects of our lives. In this exercise you have a chance to identify some of your strengths and describe how they impact your life.

Circle your strengths from the following list of choices. Add your own if you don't see any that fit you.

Wise	Fair	Creative
Artistic	Brave	Confident
Curious	Cooperative	Intelligent
Leader	Forgiving	Athletic
Empathic	Modest	Disciplined
Honest	Common sense	Assertive
Open-minded	Self-control	Logical
Persistent	Patient	Optimistic
Enthusiastic	Appreciative	Independent
Kind	Love of learning	Flexible
Loving	Humorous	Adventurous
Social	Spiritual	
Aware	Ambitious	

Describe a time one or more of your strengths made a positive difference in a relationship.

_____

_____

_____

Describe a time one or more of your strengths made a positive difference at work.

_____

_____

_____

Describe a time one or more of your strengths made a positive difference in
a community.

_____

_____

_____

Did you have any resistance to accepting that you have strengths and have used
them to make positive differences? If helpful, use a defusion technique such as
Labeling Thoughts, Sensations, Emotions, and Behaviors (page 48). This might
look like "Oh, my mind is telling me that was long ago, and I no longer have
strengths." Acknowledge the resistance and your strengths and the impact of your
strengths. Notice you can accept that both are present.

Appreciating Your Strengths

Acceptance means acknowledging and accepting life, others, and ourselves as we actually are. This means neutrally accepting our strengths as well as our vulnerabilities, the joyous moments as well as the painful ones.

Choose two to four of your favorite strengths. What makes them your favorites? Do these strengths show up in all areas of your life or do some strengths show up more in some areas?

You may notice thoughts or urges emerging, suggesting you don't have strengths. You can include them in your writing. But switch back to exploring what accepting the characteristics you value about yourself means.

_____

_____

_____

_____

_____

Sharing Strengths with Others

We often avoid being with others in response to experiencing unwanted events and emotions. We may feel shame, want to avoid being a burden, or be concerned about receiving a less than helpful response. This combination makes it easy to tiptoe into a world that does not include connection and appreciation, a world where it is easy to forget our strengths or those of others.

Choose three people from your support network and ask them to do a compliment swap with you. Explain that the compliments are about personal strengths rather than external factors such as attractiveness or possessions. Giving examples will help the strengths feel more appreciated and truer.

You may want to spend some time thinking about the strengths and stories you want to offer. If you go first, you can model a healthy appreciation style.

Accepting Your Internal Experience

Our internal experience includes our thoughts, emotions, body sensations, and behavioral urges. Most of us have learned to judge these different parts of our internal experience, often being harshly self-critical. In this subsection, you will learn to accept that these are part of your experience and do not define or limit you.

Where Did You Learn about Emotions?

Families and communities have very different approaches to emotional expression. While some treasure emotional expressiveness, others value more subtle expression. When we are under stress, emotions tend to increase and can explode or shut us down in terrifying ways.

What did you learn about emotions as a child? Are there specific memories associated with different emotions?

_____

_____

_____

_____

What have you learned about emotions as an adult? How has your experience with depression impacted your relationship with emotions?

_____

_____

_____

_____

These Feelings Belong

Our emotions bring important information about our lives and needs. They are so important that we have strong feelings about our feelings and often avoid them. Emotional avoidance keeps us stuck in the pattern of having and running from emotions. Experiencing and accepting emotions changes our relationship with them. In this practice, you will learn a tool to help you allow the feelings to be present. Read through the ideas and then practice on your own.

Take a few moments to center yourself. You might focus on the noises you hear, where and how your body is supported, or take a few mindful breathes. Make any movements that help you feel more comfortable.

Then bring to mind a difficult situation, one that evokes emotions. Notice the feelings and body sensations, any thoughts or judgments. Then place your hands on your chest and say, "These feelings belong." Allow the thoughts and feelings to continue flowing and repeat, "These feelings belong."

Your Relationship with Emotions

Most of us prefer certain emotions over others. We may try to create opportunities to experience our preferred emotions, such as watching a sad movie if we feel more comfortable with sadness than joy, or snuggling with a pet if we enjoy their companionship. These can be considered approaching an emotion, but we also tend to avoid certain emotions. For example, if we feel anxious about talking to a friend we are upset with, we may find ways to delay or prevent interacting with them, which is an example of avoiding an emotion. In this exercise, you have a chance to explore your relationship to emotions and see which you avoid and which you approach.

Name a favorite emotion.

_____

_____

_____

How do you experience that emotion? Where does it show up in your body?

_____

_____

_____

What do you like about this emotion?

_____

_____

_____

Emotions vary in level of intensity. On the scale, show the intensity level where this emotion is most enjoyable. If there is a level that you don't enjoy, mark that level with an X.

1	2	3	4	5	6	7	8	9	10
Gentle			Medium				Intense		

What do you tend to do when you experience this emotion?

_____

_____

Now name an emotion you don't like to experience.

_____

_____

What don't you like about this emotion? If there is anything you do like about it, what is it?

_____

_____

What do you tend to do when you experience this emotion?

_____

_____

On the scale, show the intensity level where this emotion is tolerable.

1	2	3	4	5	6	7	8	9	10
Gentle			Medium				Intense		

What is an emotion you see in others but don't experience yourself?

_____

_____

What do you think about this emotion?

_____

_____

What do you notice about your relationship with your emotions?

_____

_____

Most of us have been taught to manage or control our emotions. ACT teaches you to accept that emotions are part of life and to accept your feelings as they arise. What feelings arise for you at the thought of accepting your emotions?

_____

_____

_____

_____

Getting to Know the Full Palette of Emotions

Although there are hundreds of words to name emotions, neuroscientists have identified 27 different emotions based on states of arousal. They include:

1. Happiness	10. Excitement	19. Calmness
2. Sadness	11. Relief	20. Hope
3. Fear	12. Sympathy	21. Pride
4. Anger	13. Anxiety	22. Boredom
5. Surprise and dismay	14. Awkwardness	23. Envy
6. Disgust	15. Guilt	24. Confusion
7. Passionate love	16. Shame	25. Nostalgia
8. Sensory pleasure	17. Amusement	26. Craving
9. Awe	18. Pity	27. Admiration

Read through the list and notice your response to each emotion word. Then write each emotion in the boxes based on whether you generally approach, avoid, or ignore/don't have that emotion in your life.

AVOID	APPROACH	IGNORE/DON'T HAVE

Review the words in the Approach box. How is your life impacted by your decisions to approach the stimuli for these emotions?

_____

_____

_____

Review the words in the Avoid box. How is your life impacted by your decisions to avoid these emotions and the stimuli that invite them?

_____

_____

_____

Review the words in the Ignore/Don't Have box. How is your life impacted by the absence of these emotions?

_____

_____

_____

Emotions are powerful motivators to action and inaction—so powerful that they often have us acting on autopilot. Accepting that all emotions are normal responses to life and occur without needing to be obeyed, increases psychological flexibility.

Put your hand over the boxes of emotion words and say out loud, "I accept your presence in my life." Notice what emotions emerge when you do this.

Accepting the Wave

When a wave of depression moves in, you may feel hopeless about how to be with it. This worksheet invites you to notice and accept your experience.

Date: _____

Time: _____

Check the sensations and experiences you have now:

☐ Heaviness   ☐ Chest collapse   ☐ Tired/fatigue

☐ Tearfulness   ☐ Nausea   ☐ Weak

☐ Can't concentrate   ☐ Disconnected/floaty   ☐ Pain

Name any other sensations you are having.

_____

_____

_____

Show how strong the experience is now.

1	2	3	4	5	6	7	8	9	10
Mild			Moderate				Intense		

How willing are you to experience this wave of depression?

Not at all—————————————————————————Completely

Set a timer for how long you are willing to be present with the experience. You might start with three to five minutes. Feel free to set the timer for shorter or longer than that.

Allow yourself to be with this wave of depression, to notice any ebbs and flows. Notice the ways your body and mind may try to rescue you from being with this experience. Do you have a sudden urge to do something else instead? Maybe you need to go to the bathroom, make a call, or clean something. This is a rescue effort your body is making. Appreciate the parts of you trying to help you avoid this experience, and let them know you are willing to be with it right now.

When your time of being present to the experience in a focused way is up, write down what the experience of being with this wave of depression was like for you.

_____

_____

_____

_____

_____

_____

_____

_____

_____

When We Let Ourselves Down

The times when we don't live up to our expectations, or when our behaviors hurt others and ourselves, usually cause us deep pain. We can easily get caught up in, or pulled down into, spirals of guilt and shame. In this subsection, you have the chance to identify and accept these behaviors as just behaviors. You may want to include defusion practices on any that feel particularly sticky.

Regrets

Regret is a powerful emotion, one that is easy to get caught in when we are depressed. Choose an incident about which you have regret, one that you tend to revisit when depressed.

What do you most regret? In what ways did it feel like the best decision at the time? In what ways did you have misgivings about your actions?

_____

_____

How does it impact your life now? The lives of others? If you could go back in time, what would you do differently?

_____

_____

These are the questions you have likely been over numerous times. What would change in your life if you accepted the reality that, for better and for worse, you did what you did? When we struggle with the reality of consequences from something we did to ourselves or others, it helps no one. That struggle prevents our living in ways that would be helpful to us.

_____

_____

Unwanted Behaviors Checklist

Most of us have behaviors that help us avoid certain emotions, unwanted responsibilities, or various aspects of our lives. These are the behaviors that can keep us stuck in our lives. We often engage in them without noticing—like being on autopilot. Check off the unwanted behaviors you wish you didn't display.

☐ Sleeping too much

☐ Gambling

☐ Lying

☐ Cutting or harming yourself

☐ Exercising too much

☐ Unwanted sexual behaviors

☐ Using medications in ways they weren't prescribed for

☐ Not cleaning up the home

☐ Not buying or replacing needed items such as food, self-care products, clothing

☐ Skipping work or school

☐ Smoking cigarettes

☐ Telling yourself to "just get over it" or "just do it"

☐ Eating in unhealthy ways

☐ Working too much

☐ Watching too much TV

☐ Repetitive complaining

☐ Avoiding bills or opening mail

☐ _____

☐ Placing blame

☐ Avoiding healthy hygiene habits

☐ Shopping beyond your means

☐ Avoiding food

☐ Isolating from others

☐ Worrying excessively

☐ Leaving a conversation abruptly

☐ Drinking

☐ _____

Accepting ourselves means accepting that we have behaviors like the ones you checked. Accepting that you have these behaviors in the recent past does not mean accepting you will continue to do them, only that they are part of how you have been coping. What do you feel as you look at this list of behaviors?

Place one hand on the list and the other on your heart. Invite acceptance that you have done these things. Invite your observer-self to see and allow any thoughts and feelings to flow about this experience.

Creating Space

When we are emotionally overwhelmed, the tasks of keeping our home space together are frequently left undone. Many people experience shame and hopelessness when they see these constant reminders of their current struggles.

Invite your compassionate observer-self to go through your living space. Notice areas that are cluttered or dirty and any unfinished tasks. Name them out loud and complete the phrase "I see and accept that . . ." [thing you notice such as "my bed is unmade"]. Also notice and name sections that feel satisfying. This might look like "I see and accept that I put encouraging messages on the mirror." Allow emotions and thoughts to emerge, stating acceptance of those out loud as well.

Key Takeaways

The ACT process of acceptance means actively and consciously embracing your thoughts and feelings without attempting to avoid, stop, or lessen them. A few other key points we covered in this chapter were:

✓ Accepting the challenging events or internal experiences in your life frees you to be present.

✓ Accepting what is true does not mean you agree or condone it.

✓ Accepting uncomfortable emotions allows you to see them for what they are: uncomfortable emotions, often about a past experience.

CHAPTER 5

Inhabiting the Here and Now

When we are having a hard time, we may forget to nurture and comfort ourselves. This chapter will help you learn to do both by showing you how to be present in the here and now.

Our bodies, unlike our minds, do not time travel. They may recreate sensations and urges from the past or ramp up anticipating future threats, but even these are happening "now," in the moment of re-creation. This chapter will focus on helping you tune into your senses and perceptions in the body, and be more present as you engage in activities shown to impact depression: eating, sleeping, exercising, relaxing, and connecting with others.

Finding the
Doable Small Step

SANJAY DEFINED HIS DEPRESSION AS "that cycle where I am too miserable to do the thing that might make me less miserable, so I just lie there and beat myself up for being such a loser, which makes me even more miserable." Being a software engineer, he called this the "do-loop of my life, which I feel forced to repeat endlessly."

Using the Remote Control defusion activity described in chapter 3 helped Sanjay gain perspective on this pattern. He realized that he could add new "code lines" for himself. "IF I am caught in this do-loop and feel like I can't face food, THEN I can nibble on a sunflower seed." Sanjay found that slowly savoring his chosen "can't eat cycle-breaker" snack brought him back to the present. Sometimes this allowed him to notice his hunger and eat something else. He found that leaving a jar of sunflower seeds by his bed made it easier to have one, which sometimes helped him notice his hunger enough to get out of bed.

Sanjay wrote sticky notes with his new "code line" applied to other areas in his life that were impacted by depression. The sticky note "IF I feel too overwhelmed to shave, I can spray the shaving cream into my hand" sometimes helped him be present to the sensations of the shaving cream, and then be able to add the extra steps needed to shave.

Getting to Now

Psychological flexibility, that liberating in-the-moment integration of internal and external information to change or continue behavior, happens only when we are present. Yet we repeatedly get caught up in reevaluating our experiences, spending time ruminating about the past, and envisioning unwanted futures. Learning to step back from these mind traps to instead be present, is an essential part of enjoying life.

Grounding in Sound

Pick a piece of instrumental music you enjoy. Take a few moments to simply listen to it. Then, describe the piece of music as you listen. What stands out for you? What do you feel as you listen?

_____

_____

If it is not a single instrument piece, notice the different instruments. Can you focus on one separately from the others? What sounds call your attention more than others? Now notice the entirety of the music.

_____

_____

As the music ends, conduct a check of how you feel. At what points were you able to be present in the music without other thoughts distracting you?

_____

_____

Breathing to Energize

When we experience strong emotion, we tend to breath more shallowly and don't fully exhale. This can result in shortness of breath and chest tension. Longer exhales tend to bring our breath patterns back in alignment and help reduce both depression and anxiety. If focusing on breathing is difficult for you, singing and relaxing through activities such as those described in the next section are other ways to invite the breath to balance.

1. Describe your energy level and any physical sensations you feel.

    _____

    _____

    _____

    _____

2. Breathe out and make a hissing noise by pushing the air through your teeth. This activates the diaphragm at the bottom of your lungs.

3. Place your hands at the bottom of your ribs and feel the diaphragm muscles contract. Describe how this muscle contraction feels.

    _____

    _____

    _____

    _____

    Once you know how to activate these muscles, you do not need to hiss to contract them.

4. Breathe in.

5. Breathe out as long as you comfortably can.

6. Hold your breath as long as you comfortably can. Return to normal breathing.

7. Describe your energy level and any physical sensations. What changes, if any, do you notice?

Repeat steps 4 to 7 twice more and describe any changes here.

_____

_____

_____

_____

_____

_____

_____

_____

_____

_____

Hit the Pause Button

Clients often describe going through time without noticing it and later not knowing how they spent that time. Whether time is dragging on slowly or seems to be passing effortlessly, hitting the "pause button" can offer valuable information on your experience, when you are present or not so present.

1. Set a timer to ring several times a day. When it rings, stop whatever you are doing for a few minutes and answer the following questions.

2. On the scale, circle how present you were before stopping.

←	1	2	3	4	5	6	7	8	9	10	→

3. What activity were you doing when you stopped?

_____

_____

4. What position is your body in now?

_____

_____

5. What sensations is your body experiencing?

_____

_____

6. What thoughts are going through your head?

_____

_____

7. What emotions are present?

_____

_____

Now take a few deep breaths, using the technique you just learned or one you learned in this book or elsewhere.

Do you want to return to the activity you were doing before pausing? If so, invite being more aware of living in the moment as you continue with your activity.

If you don't want to return to that activity, choose one that feels right for you and begin it with awareness. The next exercise invites you to notice how changes in activities impact your ability to be present to your experience.

Use this tool several times a day. At the end of a day, reflect on how stopping to notice your activities and experiences impacts your choices about how you spend your time.

What Interferes with Being Present?

Being and staying present is often difficult, and most of us have many invitations and habits that make it even more challenging. In the following list, check the items interfering with you being present. Where there are lines, indicate the specific ones that impact you.

☐ Sense of worry

☐ Heavy mood

☐ Specific worries:

_____

☐ Preoccupation with body image

☐ Cravings:

_____

☐ Numbness, deadness

☐ Sense of urgency or panic

☐ Spacing out while watching shows or playing apps and games

☐ Reaching out to others

☐ Taking on new tasks

☐ Multitasking

☐ Sleeping

☐ Others

_____

_____

_____

In the chart, choose a few of your checked items to re-attempt them in a way that allows you to be more present. Record your results. The first two lines show examples to help get you started.

INTERFERES WITH BEING PRESENT	CHANGE	RESULT
Zoning on an app	*Play with friend or try VR version*	*The VR keeps me focused in the now. Playing with a friend was fun, but I felt anxious sometimes.*

INTERFERES WITH BEING PRESENT	CHANGE	RESULT
Numbness	*Do exercise to be present to numbness, for example, try Accepting the Wave (page 82)*	*I could feel the numbness in my chest—I never thought about it as a feeling.*

Hello Body

For many people, depression creates a sense of distance or remoteness from their body. We can become estranged from our bodies as we experience the various challenges of life: illness, loss, overwork, social and physical threats. Depression can pull us toward thoughts, memories, or feelings that disconnect us from contact with the world, including the important signals from our body that carry both our sadness and joys. Our bodies carry the exhaustion, pain, grief, and anxiety from these challenges as well as demands for food and fluid, sleep, exercise, and touch with others. Reconnecting with your body is a key step in living in the present. This section provides activities to help you reconnect with your body.

Favorite Moments with Your Body

What are the favorite times you have known with your body? These often happen when we are "in the zone"—fully present and vibrant within our bodies. If you are or have been athletic, what moments of participating in your sport come to mind? If you enjoy art or the act of creation, what moments of witnessing or creating stand out for you? Times of designing and building projects? Of close connection and intimacy with another? Of relaxing and being at peace?

_____

_____

_____

_____

_____

_____

_____

Body Inventory

Circle the words from the list that describe any physical sensations you are currently having. There are spaces for you to add any other sensations you are feeling. Next, on the body image that follows, label with your selected words indicating where you experience that sensation.

Pressure	Choking	Cold
Numb	Sluggish	Burning
Pain	Prickly	Hot
Relaxed	Still	Heavy
Twisted	Comfortable	_____
Strong	Tense	_____
Peaceful	Pins and needles	_____
Straight	Compacted	_____
Centered	Buzzing	_____
Loose	Aching	_____
Shaking	Dead	_____
Agony	Quiet	_____
Agitated	Shivering	
Frazzled	Weak	
Alive	Restless	
Languid	Racing	
Light	Tight	
Calm	Bubbly	

_____   _____
_____   _____
_____   _____
_____   _____
_____   _____
_____   _____
_____   _____
_____   _____
_____   _____

What do you notice as you feel your body overall?

_____

_____

_____

What sensations are you curious about?

_____

_____

_____

Moving with Your Breath

In this exercise, you will observe your body as you sit and allow your breathing to guide your body's movements. Modify the suggestions to adjust for any physical limitations you may have. The goal is to be in touch with your body gently and safely.

Before you begin, describe how your body feels.

_____

_____

_____

_____

_____

How relaxed do you feel? Note it on the chart.

| ← | 1 | 2 | 3 | 4 | 5 | 6 | 7 | 8 | 9 | 10 | → |

Notice the parts of you that are touching the floor, or a chair, or the bed. Wiggle your toes and pelvic area to settle in more fully. Allow yourself to relax, moving gently to release any tension.

Exhale deeply, then invite a deep breath in and allow your body to move with the inhale, then the exhale. Continue breathing for five to six breaths as you let your body expand and contract.

Notice the vertebrae in your back, moving together to create space for the air. Allow the ripple of movement to extend to your head. Your head may curl forward as you exhale and rock back as you inhale. Explore different movements: shifting shoulders, rolling your head left to right, making circles with your arms.

After a few minutes, let your breathing return to normal.

Describe in writing how your body feels.

_____

_____

_____

_____

_____

How relaxed do you feel, one being entirely unrelaxed and ten being totally relaxed? Note it on the chart.

| ← | 1 | 2 | 3 | 4 | 5 | 6 | 7 | 8 | 9 | 10 | → |

Emotions in Your Body

When you feel anxious, do you notice it anywhere in your body? Some people describe tension in their chest or stomach discomfort when they feel anxious. Is what you feel similar or something else when you are anxious? What about sadness? Where do you feel that in your body?

When researchers asked people to associate body sensations with emotional triggers, they found strong consistency and used the information to create the emotion maps shown (Nummenmaa et al., 2014). Choose an emotion shown in the following image that best aligns with your own experience. Then, in the second graphic, make your own map of your emotions. The Body Inventory activity on page 99 may help you complete this activity.

The ability to link our body sensations to our emotions can help us be more aware and accepting of them.

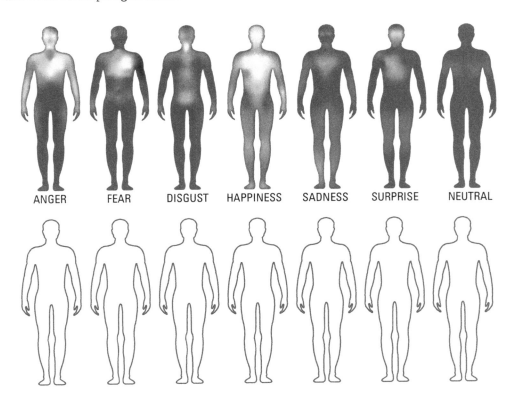

ANGER FEAR DISGUST HAPPINESS SADNESS SURPRISE NEUTRAL

Create a Grounding Kit

Having access to simple tools that help you return to the present moment can be extremely helpful. Make these tools available at home and in a travel kit. The table below suggests items by primary sensory experience that may help keep you grounded. You may find some items that activate more than one sense, such as scented stress balls. You can find websites that offer items shown to help with depression and anxiety, such as weighted blankets or vests, in the Resources section on page 204.

PRIMARY SENSE	ITEMS YOU MIGHT WANT TO TEST	NOTES
Touch	smooth stones fidget toys and jewelry cloth scraps to touch or twist stress balls small craft items	
Sound	recorded meditations recorded music finger harps harmonicas	
Visual	patterned cloth photos or images set of pencils and small notebook	
Smell	fruits such as oranges herbs such as rosemary or mint tea bags essential oils	
Taste	small fruits, such as berries, dried fruit	
Movement	small balls or bags to toss in the air yo-yos music to dance or to work out	

Smart devices are also excellent sources of auditory, visual, and tactile options that can ground or distract.

Welcoming Nutrition

Changes in appetite are one of the classic challenges of depression, often resulting in significant weight gain or loss. You may feel intense cravings for certain foods and find yourself eating ravenously even though your stomach is full. You might experience nausea at the mere thought of food and go long periods of time without eating. Some people describe being unaware that they are hungry, that they do not notice the cues their body gives. Patterns like these may be experienced at different times.

Claim Your Crunchies

Finding foods that are satisfying, meet your dietary needs, and also have nutritional value can be daunting. Crunchy foods often top the satisfaction list, so in this exercise, you get to savor and compare different crunchy snacks. If creamy is your satisfaction go-to, feel free to do that instead of or in addition to the crunchy options.

Set up five crunchy items you might find pleasure eating. Include different categories: chips, crackers, nuts, veggie sticks, fruit, cereal. Explore each item and write your observations on the snack bags.

Colors _____

_____

Shape _____

_____

Smell _____

_____

Taste: sour, sweet, salty, bitter, spicy _____

_____

How loud is the crunch?

← 1 2 3 4 5 6 7 8 9 10 →

How satisfying is the snack?

← 1 2 3 4 5 6 7 8 9 10 →

How present were you when exploring this snack?

← 1 2 3 4 5 6 7 8 9 10 →

Colors _____

_____

Shape _____

_____

Smell _____

_____

Taste: sour, sweet, salty, bitter, spicy _____

_____

How loud is the crunch?

| ← | 1 | 2 | 3 | 4 | 5 | 6 | 7 | 8 | 9 | 10 | → |

How satisfying is the snack?

| ← | 1 | 2 | 3 | 4 | 5 | 6 | 7 | 8 | 9 | 10 | → |

How present were you exploring this snack?

| ← | 1 | 2 | 3 | 4 | 5 | 6 | 7 | 8 | 9 | 10 | → |

Colors _____

_____

Shape _____

_____

Smell _____

_____

Taste: sour, sweet, salty, bitter, spicy _____

_____

How loud is the crunch?

| ← | 1 | 2 | 3 | 4 | 5 | 6 | 7 | 8 | 9 | 10 | → |

How satisfying is the snack?

| ← | 1 | 2 | 3 | 4 | 5 | 6 | 7 | 8 | 9 | 10 | → |

How present were you when exploring this snack?

| ← | 1 | 2 | 3 | 4 | 5 | 6 | 7 | 8 | 9 | 10 | → |

Colors _____

_____

Shape _____

_____

Smell _____

_____

Taste: sour, sweet, salty, bitter, spicy _____

_____

How loud is the crunch?

| ← | 1 | 2 | 3 | 4 | 5 | 6 | 7 | 8 | 9 | 10 | → |

How satisfying is the snack?

| ← | 1 | 2 | 3 | 4 | 5 | 6 | 7 | 8 | 9 | 10 | → |

How present were you when exploring this snack?

| ← | 1 | 2 | 3 | 4 | 5 | 6 | 7 | 8 | 9 | 10 | → |

Colors _____

_____

Shape _____

_____

Smell _____

_____

Taste: sour, sweet, salty, bitter, spicy _____

_____

How loud is the crunch?

←	1	2	3	4	5	6	7	8	9	10	→

How satisfying is the snack?

←	1	2	3	4	5	6	7	8	9	10	→

How present were you when exploring this snack?

←	1	2	3	4	5	6	7	8	9	10	→

If overeating is a pattern, would mindfully eating one of these snacks help you stay present and only eat the amount you want to? Conversely, if there are times you struggle to eat, would mindfully snacking allow you to eat?

A Mindful Meal

One of depression's signature symptoms is its impact on appetite, either by depleting or increasing it. While we may often eat mindlessly or compulsively, the sensory richness of food allows it to be a satisfying living-in-the-moment experience. Here are some ideas to welcome being more present at a meal, whether it is fast food at a crowded desk or a sumptuous feast at a beautifully set table. Review these suggestions and make it a goal to put them into practice during at least one meal this week.

1. Be hungry but not ravenous. Have a snack before the meal if you haven't eaten for a while.

2. If you eat with others, agree to avoid stressful topics and behaviors during the meal.

3. Center yourself before beginning to eat. Observe the room and the presentation of the food, anyone who is with you.

4. Take a moment to appreciate the efforts of those who make the meal possible, from farmers and transportation providers to food sellers and preparers. If any of them are present, including yourself, thank them.

5. Take small bites and savor the food with all your senses. Notice the various textures, colors, patterns, tastes, and sounds. Be aware of the thoughts and feelings that occur as you do.

6. Pause and put down your silverware between bites. Do you detect any changes in your hunger level and body satisfaction?

7. Take a moment at the end of the meal to reflect on what has changed.

Rest, Relaxation, and Sleep

Sleep is one of the primary areas impacted by depression, and being deprived of restful sleep makes life much more difficult. Being present to your body's current state and mental activity levels can help you both allow relaxation and sleep to occur and to decide when seeking sleep is helpful.

Relaxing into Sleep

Bring this workbook with you to your sleeping place and read through the steps. The first few times you try it, you may need to refer to the steps. Make adjustments as necessary to help you relax and fall asleep.

1. Choose a comfortable place to relax, one where you won't be disturbed for a while. Collect any pillows or covers that will help you be more comfortable.

2. Lie or sit in a way that helps you feel supported and safe. Add small pillows or rolled towels under your knees, ankles, or neck—any of the places that support your body and allow you to relax more deeply.

3. Breathe out as long as you comfortably can. Open your mouth and invite a yawn as you breathe in. Notice how your body feels, where it is relaxed and where it is tense. Wiggle any areas that are tense: shoulders, hips, neck. Notice any softening of your body and thank it for relaxing.

4. If any distressing thoughts arise, acknowledge that your mind is having thoughts and return to noticing your body.

5. Take note of the back of your body. Let it soften.

6. Focus on the front of your body and allow any tension to soften. Gently wiggle any areas that need it.

7. Acknowledge your body, resting here in this moment. Experience it.

8. Check if your body feels ready to sleep. Be open to what your body wants. Allow yourself to relax a little more.

9. Continue resting, feeling your body relax, perhaps tense up and relax again. Be present with your body, listening to the patterns of tension, release, and relaxation.

Should I Stay in Bed Now?

Sleep specialists recommend being in bed only for sleep or intimacy and encourage leaving the bed if you are unable to fall asleep within half an hour. This applies to both the initial falling asleep and falling back asleep if you've woken up before you have had enough sleep.

Keeping a sleep diary is a helpful start. Start with how many hours of sleep you want each day. Write the clock time for sleep and wake times (your best guess is fine) and total the hours for each chunk of sleep. Evaluate how restful each sleep chunk is on a scale of 1 to 5.

SUNDAY	
Hours of sleep desired	
Total time in sleeping spot	
Total hours/minutes of sleep	
How restful	
Notes	
MONDAY	
Hours of sleep desired	
Total time in sleeping spot	
Total hours/minutes of sleep	
How restful	
Notes	

TUESDAY	
Hours of sleep desired	
Total time in sleeping spot	
Total hours/minutes of sleep	
How restful	
Notes	

WEDNESDAY	
Hours of sleep desired	
Total time in sleeping spot	
Total hours/minutes of sleep	
How restful	
Notes	

THURSDAY	
Hours of sleep desired	
Total time in sleeping spot	
Total hours/minutes of sleep	
How restful	
Notes	

FRIDAY	
Hours of sleep desired	
Total time in sleeping spot	
Total hours/minutes of sleep	
How restful	
Notes	
SATURDAY	
Hours of sleep desired	
Total time in sleeping spot	
Total hours/minutes of sleep	
How restful	
Notes	

How many hours are you spending in bed when you aren't asleep but are trying to sleep or wishing you were asleep? What is your experience during those times of unwanted wakefulness?

_____

_____

Being present to your body's energy and your mind's activity level when you are seeking sleep can help in several ways. The observing-self can label thoughts and accept feelings and sensations. Both can be calming. The observing-self can also help you decide when the energy levels are too high for sleep to come and that moving to a different part of your living space is recommended. If we spend sleepless hours frustrated that we can't sleep in our bed, we come to associate our bed with that experience. Describe the patterns that help you decide to leave your bed instead of continuing to seek sleep and feel frustrated.

Connecting with Others

Depression and isolation go hand in hand. People often isolate when they feel down, a pattern that might protect us from more rejection but can also strengthen fusion and hopelessness. In this subsection, you get to explore your internal experiences around connecting with others.

Connecting with a Photo

Select a photo of a friend or family member you would like to have a better relationship with. Spend a few minutes with the photo before you start to write. What do you notice about them in the photo? Notice any thoughts and feelings you have as you look at their image.

Now write about how you currently feel while looking at this photo and using defusion language from chapter 3 (page 43). For example, you might write, "My heart stirs when I see their eyes and smile and I feel myself wanting to call them." Or "My mind is reminding me of that time they didn't come by when they said they would, and my eyes tear up."

_____

_____

_____

_____

_____

_____

_____

Practice Your Listening Skills

Just as we get pulled into negative thought patterns and emotional reactions to our thoughts and experiences, we can have the same behaviors when listening to others. People often describe planning what they will say rather than listening to understand the other person's experience. Being present to and accepting of your own internal experience while they talk can free you to understand and relate to them more deeply.

This week, choose someone who will be open to you exploring a different way of interacting with them. What helps you understand their viewpoint better? How might you feel if you were in their circumstance? Do they seem to feel similarly to how you believe you might feel?

Think of the emotions and urges that arise as you listen. Do you want to help them? Avoid them or their situation? Take charge and "fix" the situation for them? Accept your feelings and urges without acting on them, then return to listening attentively.

You may want to make supportive comments or ask open-ended follow-up questions.

How does it feel to listen to another person in this way? Ask the other person how the experience was for them.

Exploring What Builds Closeness

This exercise is for you to complete with someone you would like to become closer with. It can be a family member, friend, colleague, or romantic partner.

Gary Chapman, PhD, is a well-known couple's therapist who wrote the popular book *The Five Love Languages: How to Express Heartfelt Commitment to Your Mate*. Although his focus was on strengthening romantic relationships, there are other ways to think about how we behave in supportive relationships; the caring behavior patterns he identifies as love languages are relevant to healthy relationships.

If you are working with someone you've known for a while, you can recall times when you each did the caring behavior for the other or explore new ways of giving to each other. With someone new, you can try them out.

You as Giver

CARING BEHAVIOR	WHAT YOU DID OR SAID	YOUR EXPERIENCE	THEIR EXPERIENCE
Words of affirmation			
Acts of service			
Gifts			
Quality time			
Wanted physical touch			

You as Receiver

CARING BEHAVIOR	WHAT THEY DID OR SAID	YOUR EXPERIENCE	THEIR EXPERIENCE
Words of affirmation			
Acts of service			
Gifts			
Quality time			
Wanted physical touch			

Creating Oases in Time and Space

Managing time and organizing space are complex tasks that often become overwhelming. Once we get behind on either, the effects can be yet more overwhelming and make being present even less inviting. In this section, you get to choose a few grounding anchors that help you be present more often.

A Centering Small Change

Living in a space that feels cluttered and filled with unopened mail, unwashed dishes, and unpaid bills feels overwhelming and invites self-condemnation and hopelessness. It is also a common reality for people going through a difficult time. The goal of this exercise is to help you identify a small, doable change that will bring relief and centeredness. It might be as simple as wiping the stove top each night and setting up things for your favorite morning beverage or skimming the mail to pull out the bills that would have unwanted consequences if left unpaid.

With the following list, rank any unfinished task area by how much stress and shame they cause you (1 to 5 with 5 being the highest).

Laundry	Bathroom cleanliness	Unopened mail
Dishes	Unpaid bills	Unopened email
Lack of food	Trash piling up	Decayed food
Clutter	Dirt, grime	Insects or rodents
Other _____		

Pick one of your most stressful tasks, what sights/sounds/smells trouble you the most?

_____

_____

_____

What about this issue interferes with your quality and ease of life? How does it impact you?

_____

_____

_____

_____

What small change can you do mindfully each day that will feel like a gift to experience? For example, straightening the covers in the morning so I see one clear surface and know the covers will stay on me better.

_____

_____

_____

_____

Finding Your Personal Anchor

Are there movements that help you center? Some people find touching a certain object helps center them. For others, it is placing their hand on their heart. For me, it is noticing the soles of my feet touching the ground. I've had various medical conditions and injuries that left me unable to walk for periods of time and prognoses that I would not walk again. I remember my mother and husband rubbing my feet to reduce the pain. Noticing the soles of my feet on the ground roots me to my mother's and husband's love and to the reality that good things happen even when I don't know how to make them happen.

What holds meaning for you and can become your personal anchor in the here and now?

_____

_____

_____

_____

_____

_____

_____

_____

_____

Key Takeaways

Being present is one of the key processes ACT teaches to promote psychological flexibility. In this chapter, you were introduced to a variety of ways to live in the here and now. You had the chance to apply these skills in the areas where being present can be challenging while in the grip of depression. The areas of being present to the body experience and emotions and to the areas of eating, sleeping, interactions with others, and unwanted behaviors were covered in this chapter because they are frequently impacted by depression.

✓ The body lives in the present. Sights, sounds, smells, tastes, and sensations are steady invitations to the here and now.

✓ When you are overwhelmed or caught up in thoughts and judgments, noticing sensory experiences can ground you.

✓ You can anticipate times and places where you are most likely to get stuck and set up sensory invitations to invite you gently back to the present.

✓ Being present to our physical sensations, emotions, thoughts, and behaviors allows us to accept them for what they are.

CHAPTER 6

Understanding Yourself and Your Life in a New Way

You may have felt in the earlier chapters that you are more than your thoughts, feelings, and internal experiences; that there is a part of you that can observe, step back from, and even accept the elements of your experience. In ACT, this part of you is often called the observer-self.

You may also have noticed that your thoughts often depict you a certain way: I am weak, no one cares about me, etc. ACT identifies this part as the conceptualized-self. The third aspect of self that ACT describes is the ongoing process of self-awareness, the part that can live in the zone of psychological flexibility.

In this chapter, you will have chances to strengthen your connection with your observer-self, to learn to experience your life story freer from your conceptualized model of self, and explore tools to help you be present to the fullness of your life as it is.

Celebrating
Love after Death

"**EVEN WHEN I'M GOING ON** a walk and can see it is a lovely day, I don't feel any-thing," Laura told me. "It's as though there is a wall between myself and the world, even when I'm doing what is supposed to help." Laura's daughter, Sandra, had died four years prior. Sandra was only 27 when the ovarian cancer diagnosis came as she and her husband had not become pregnant after a year of trying. Despite grief counseling and efforts to carry on for the family, Laura's heart remained locked in sorrow.

Laura's husband and other children were asking if she could return to them or if they had to accept that they had lost her as well. When they said she went through the right motions but wasn't present, Laura acknowledged they were right. She could recognize the same pattern but did not know how to change it.

Laura began to observe and be present to her numbness. As she explored this natural protective device, she began to notice that other feelings lay beneath it. Writing the story of losing her daughter helped face the tragic loss for herself and the individual members of the extended family. Slowly, she became able to grieve more fully, to be present to the anguish she felt and the sense of injustice. As Laura did, she was more able to experience the memories and cherish them. She and the family began talking about the loss of their cherished Sandra and to find ways to celebrate her life. While she continued to miss and grieve Sandra, Laura was able to be present to those feelings and to connect more fully with other aspects of her life and her family.

Learning to Kindly Observe Your Inner Experience

Allowing our observer-self to witness the steady flow of inner experience helps by creating space and perspective. Our internal experience can be seen as the valuable source of information that it is, rather than as facts that must be reacted to.

Identifying Myths about Emotions

Myths often shut down the natural flow of emotions by reinforcing the fear of them. Identifying which myths you were taught can help your observer-self recognize them more readily for what they are: myths, not facts. Keeping that in mind, check the box by the myths that sound familiar.

- ☐ If I talk about my feelings, others will think I am weak.
- ☐ Feeling these negative emotions means I am a bad, weak person.
- ☐ If I let myself grieve, I will fall apart and be sad forever.
- ☐ Emotions are dangerous.

- ☐ No one else feels as bad as I do. I'm broken.
- ☐ I will become suicidal if I let myself feel sad.
- ☐ Wallowing in negative emotions is for losers.
- ☐ Feelings come out of nowhere with no warning.

- ☐ Only immature people and "drama queens" have strong emotions.
- ☐ I don't have time to feel this.
- ☐ If people knew how I feel, they wouldn't want to be my friend.

Next, choose three of the myths you checked and challenge them. Here is an example.

If I talk about my emotions, people will think I am weak.

It's true that people who don't know how to deal with their own emotions might believe this myth about emotions being a sign of weakness. But I don't want to be like them. I'm learning to accept that emotions are a natural, healthy part of life and healing and that avoiding them causes more problems than experiencing and accepting them.

Greet the Feeling

Often, when we ignore our emotions, they get larger and more intrusive until we can do nothing else but accept that they need our attention. A friend put it well, "Depression is like my dog. If I ignore it, it gets so demanding I can't work or focus on anything. If I play with my dog and give it some attention, it will let me focus on the other parts of my life."

Describe some of the ways your sadness acts up to get your attention. How does your sadness change when you make space for it, perhaps allowing tears to flow or some form of comfort to be received?

_____

_____

_____

_____

_____

_____

Noticing When You Notice

Sit comfortably and take a few deep breathes. Be aware of yourself sitting there and being present, witnessing the thoughts, emotions, and physical sensations that are part of now. What changes do you notice in your body as you sit and focus? What thought is your mind thinking? How would you characterize your observer-self?

Notice how you experience the observing-self as separate from these, then journal about the experience of being with your observing-self.

Core Beliefs as Part of Our Contextualized Self

When we go through challenging experiences without enough support, especially as children, we can develop negative core beliefs about ourselves. The two main categories of negative core beliefs that drive depression are those about being unlovable or helpless. These become part of our conceptualized self, the identity we develop around our unresolved wounds.

Circle the words from each list that you often feel are true about you.

Unlovable Core Beliefs

Bad

Unlovable

Different (bad)

Unattractive

Uncared for

Not good enough

Unworthy

Unlikable

Unwanted

Going to be abandoned

Going to be rejected

Going to be alone

Helpless Core Beliefs

Powerless

Ineffective

Vulnerable

Helpless

Needy

Trapped

Defective

Incompetent

Not good enough

Weak

Out of control

Inadequate

Pick one of the previously mentioned core beliefs that hurt you.

_____

_____

How did you learn this belief?

_____

_____

_____

How true does the belief feel in this moment? Note it on the chart, with 10 being the most true.

| ← | 1 | 2 | 3 | 4 | 5 | 6 | 7 | 8 | 9 | 10 | → |

Choose one of the defusion techniques from chapter 3 to practice on this belief.

_____

_____

_____

Are there times where you felt the opposite of the negative core belief, either loved or competent?

_____

_____

_____

If so, describe one of those times.

_____

_____

_____

How true does the negative core belief feel in this moment?

| ← | 1 | 2 | 3 | 4 | 5 | 6 | 7 | 8 | 9 | 10 | → |

How can your observer-self use this information to protect you better from this false belief?

_____

_____

_____

Let the Tangle Become the Weave

In day-to-day and especially workplace conversation, the expectation is that we will "stick to the topic" instead of following the course of our thoughts and emotions. Yet our inner worlds are rich compilations of sensations, urges, thoughts, and feelings that blend memory, current awareness, and possibilities. My friend and colleague, MaryAnn Gutoff, says that perspective, a gift of our observer-self, allows us to see "either a tangle or a weave."

We must sit gently with our pain and allow the feelings, thoughts, sensations, and urges to unravel and crisscross through years and various experiences, shifting from rage to sorrow as needed to heal us.

Choose a loss or difficult experience that troubles you. Set a timer for ten to fifteen minutes and allow your inner experience about the loss to flow. Let your observer-self track the various streams that flow and invite you back to that flow if distractions invite you away.

Once the timer goes off, allow time to notice what themes or patterns emerged from the tangle. On the lines below, record your thoughts on what emerged during this time. Describe any symbols, feelings, sensations or behavioral urges you feel called to.

_____

_____

_____

_____

_____

_____

Welcoming the Good

When we are caught in the turmoil of emotions or deadening numbness ignited by loss, it can seem impossible to remember feeling close with anyone. Our brains select the negative to help us survive. With practice, positive experiences can be remembered and strengthened.

Find a comfortable position. Exhale deeply. Think of a moment when you felt love or happiness with someone. You can choose a family member, friend, pet, fictional character, anyone. Place a hand over your heart. Allow yourself to remember the experience. Notice any changes in your feelings and body. When ready, write about the feelings and memory.

_____

_____

_____

_____

_____

_____

_____

_____

_____

_____

Coming to Terms with Your Life

Life includes profound losses and terrifying threats, both of which throw our lives off the course we imagined. Until we learn to access our observing-self, these events can easily become part of our fused definition of self and identity. Learning to witness and accept the internal experience of these losses and threats frees us to know we are more than these experiences and the wreckage they leave.

Dreams Delayed or Lost

The losses and challenges we experience in life often alter the course of our lives permanently. Medical conditions may impact career choices and social opportunities. A job loss may lead to homelessness or require a move to a different region or country. Those we lose to death or estrangement remain gone, year after year.

What losses have you experienced in your life that are difficult to accept? How do the losses alter your life today? What would be different if you accepted this as it was, without fighting against this piece of your past?

_____

_____

_____

_____

_____

_____

_____

Understanding Grief

Grief is the complex response we have to any major loss, not only the death of someone important. We grieve the life that would have been after a diagnosis, a job loss, a move to another community or country. We grieve the loss of trust when we are hurt by others. Grieving is both a process and a skill. Learning how to grieve well helps us move from overwhelm and psychological rigidity to finding peace and going forward with satisfying lives.

J. William Worden describes four Tasks of Mourning in his book *Grief Counseling and Grief Therapy*. For this exercise, choose a significant loss in your life you can use to help you explore the following tasks.

1. The first task is accepting the reality of the loss. In what ways do you accept the reality of this loss? In what ways do you fight accepting it?

_____

_____

_____

_____

2. The second task involves working though the painful emotions of grieving this loss. In what ways have you allowed yourself time and space to experience the emotions? In what ways are you deferring or avoiding the painful emotions? How has this changed with time?

_____

_____

_____

_____

3. The third task is adjusting to the world without the person, health, or situation. What adjustments have you made, willingly or because you had no choice? What adjustments are too painful to face? Why? What about these adjustments blocks you?

_____

_____

_____

_____

_____

4. The final task is finding a new relationship with who or what you lost. If someone moved away, it might mean changing from a local relationship to a long-distance one. In the case of medical disability, it might mean being able to remember the former strength and possibilities with fondness.

_____

_____

_____

_____

_____

Inviting Acceptance

Acceptance of change, particularly loss, is usually a slow process that leads to a new way of being. Although it is simple to state we accept something, actually integrating acceptance of an unwanted change requires time to slowly become more real. This exercise allows you to invite acceptance of one of the more difficult areas of your life and to notice and accept your experience of the loss as it is now.

Complete the following concept map about one of your major losses. You could use your diagnosis and reality of living with depression.

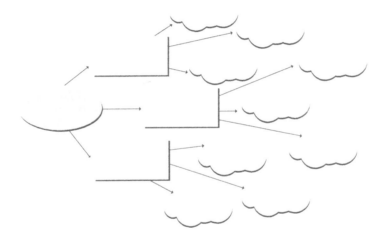

Complete the thought: If I were to accept that [name either a reality you have that is difficult to accept, or a loss you have suffered in the center circle], it would mean that [list the thoughts that arise in the boxes].

Add any body sensations (in the circle) and emotions (in the clouds) that go with the thoughts.

Then, place one hand over the page and the other over your heart. Say out loud, "I accept that this is part of my reality and that these are the thoughts and feelings I experience about it now. I accept these parts of my experience, even if I choose not to believe or act on them."

Invite tenderness for yourself, facing this unwanted situation and the many thoughts, emotions, and sensations that you experience about it. Say out loud, "I am more than this situation and this experience of it."

Holding Your Grief

Deep losses wreak havoc in our lives, rip apart our sense of self and purpose and often leave us feeling alone and defeated. Nothing prepares us for the depth and range of painful emotions that shift and change or freeze and refuse to budge. Sorrow, anger, numbness, guilt, longing, anguish, and betrayal are all part of *healthy* grief. Even though others may mourn the same loss, each person will have their own unique experience. Learning how to be with the emotions, to allow them to flow through and resolve takes time and experimentation.

When you can find others to share the grief with, it helps put the pain in perspective and affirm that, yes, others go through this also. You may be able to find support groups for your specific loss in the community or online. Finding ways that allow you to be with the emotions at the right level for a given moment will help. Next is a list of options. Check the ones you have tried and found helpful. Star the ones you might want to try.

Music that allows you to feel deeply:

☐ Listening to songs

☐ Singing

☐ Playing an instrument

☐ Writing songs

Images that connect you to who or what you lost:

☐ Looking at photos

☐ Creating scrapbooks or presentations

☐ Creating art: drawing, painting, etc.

☐ Watching movies that reflect similar losses

Words honoring love and loss:

☐ Reading books, poems, essays

☐ Writing letters, poems, essays, books

☐ Listening to others speak

Rituals, social grieving:

☐ Attending a funeral, memorial, or celebration of life

☐ Sitting shiva

☐ Arranging for a ritual honoring the deceased

☐ Spending time grieving with others

Now that you've reviewed your options, choose one to spend the next few minutes doing. Remember to be patient with yourself and allow the feelings to flow as long as they need to. Losses take time to process and accept.

Adjusting to Your World Post-Loss

When we have a major loss, whether it be death, divorce, a breakup, or relocation, the day-to-day fabric of our lives has significant gaps and often remnants of what once was. One significant task of mourning is adjusting to these gaps and finding our way to cope with the remnants. In this exercise, you will name a significant loss and identify the changes it created in your current life. Choose a loss that impacts you the most, whether it is the loss of a job or community, your health, a person.

Naming the Loss

On _____ [date], I lost _____ [name], my _____ [role or title] to _____ [cause of loss]. My identifying role changed from

_____ to _____. This loss leaves the following holes and needs

adjustments in my life:

AREA	HOLE LEFT	ADJUSTMENT NEEDED
Homelife		
Healthcare		
Personal care		
Financial situation		
Recreation		

Acknowledging the missing areas in your life is an essential though painful part of mourning. What adjustments do you need to make? What have you already done? Everyone grieves at their own pace. Be gentle with yourself. As you grieve, listen for where you may be ready to make an adjustment.

Creating a New Relationship with Your Losses

Our hearts and memories do not stop reaching for someone or a community because they are dead or missing. We are left to define a new relationship with them as we go forward without them.

Writing or talking to our missing person helps people grieve and go forward. Write a letter or journal entry that includes some of the following:

1. *Thank you for* . . . [Name and describe what you appreciate about them and the relationship].

2. *I forgive or want to forgive you for* . . . [Name the places where you feel hurt or betrayed by that person's choices or behaviors]. Forgiveness, like acceptance, does not mean what happened is okay. Emotional forgiveness means you release the anger and resentment so that you do not need to carry it any longer.

3. *Please forgive me for* . . . [Express your remorse to them for any actions, thoughts, or feelings you regret]. Grieving often includes significant guilt about things done and left undone, things said and left unsaid.

4. Close with your feelings about them.

This letter or journal entry is for you. If the person or community you lost is still living, this version is not for their eyes. Be present with your internal experience long enough to find peace around the loss before considering what you might want to communicate to them directly.

Graphic Novel Page of You in the Zone

Bit by bit, the observing-self—and allowing thoughts and feelings, urges and sensations to flow through us without defining us—will create moments of time when we can experience psychological flexibility. We can remain, or readily return to being, in the present after we encounter situations or people that invite us back into fusion and negative self-definition. You can do this exercise in real time and use the following graphic novel template to record your experience, or you can just visualize it.

Go for a walk, bike ride, drive, or commute to places where it will be relatively easy to stay in the present. Go to at least one place where there will be things that remind you of a significant loss you have been working through. On the graphic novel template that follows, draw the trip you've taken. Add comments in the word and thought bubbles to accept the moments you are present, the decisions you make, and how you respond to the thoughts and feelings that pull you away from the present.

Key Takeaways

In this chapter, you've learned about the three different aspects of self in ACT, and tasks that can help you process a loss to move from psychological rigidity to flexibility. We start from our conceptualized-self and, with the aid of the observing-self, move toward living within each moment as the context changes around and within us.

✓ The conceptualized-self is built around our physical realities, such as age and physical attributes, as well as the identification with our life history.

✓ The observing-self is the part that witnesses internal experiences of thoughts, feelings, sensations, and behavioral urges, as well as external events.

✓ The self-as-context allows us to process experiences in life moment by moment, in the context of our current situation and our internal experience of it. As we continue developing these skills, we can more often notice when we are caught up in our conceptualized-self and invite ourselves to be present to the circumstances we are facing in the moment.

CHAPTER 7

Clarifying What Matters to You

O ur values, by definition, mean a great deal to us. When we are living according to our values, we tend to be happier and have more energy and creativity. The opposite is also true. The areas and ways we are not living by our values tend to cause discomfort and even anguish.

Our core values express our deepest desires about how we want to live in the world. Core values tend to be present in all areas of our lives. For example, someone who values integrity may express it differently in personal relationships than they do in their work relationships, yet it remains essential in both. The same person may have different values in each domain or area of their lives. For example, someone who values order in their financial affairs may value spontaneity when they create art or decide how to enjoy time off. This chapter will help you explore and find your core values and the life area values that will guide you in creating a rich and satisfying life.

Not So Little Lies

GEOFFREY STRUGGLED WITH BOTH DEPRESSION and PTSD. He was raised by a single mother who beat and belittled him when she was drunk and rageful. School had been a sanctuary, so he learned to excel there as a child, and then at work as an adult. He alternated between periods of intense activity and times when he withdrew from the world.

Geoff found himself calming down and letting go of many unwanted behaviors as he learned to experience his feelings and accept the events of his life. Even before he defined his values in therapy, Geoff lived by his deeply held core values of integrity and honesty. The ways he lived by these core values positively impacted both his personal relationships and professional world, despite his times of avoiding everyone.

When he felt threatened, one of his default behaviors was lying before he realized it. Feeling ashamed, he would then tell more extensive lies to cover up the initial lie. For example, if he was late because he overslept, he would say he was late because the cat escaped the house. Then he would embellish the story with many details that showed him in a favorable light. Being caught in one of these lie spirals was extremely painful, and the remorse he felt often precipitated one of his withdrawal periods. When he returned from one of these, he would not acknowledge the lie but just try to go forward.

Defining his values of integrity and honesty helped him decide to bring up, and begin to work on, his lying pattern. The first steps were accepting that he had this pattern and to invite compassion and understanding for how the pattern developed.

Exploring Your Core Values

Core values underlie our lives, both in how we follow those values and the pain we experience when we don't. This subsection includes activities to help you explore your values, how they formed, and where they show up in your life now.

If I Weren't Depressed

Do you ever wonder what your life would be like if you weren't depressed? What would your life look like if you had enough energy to do the things you want? If you felt comfortable going out and connecting with people, how would your life change? Write about this on the following lines.

_____

_____

_____

_____

_____

_____

_____

_____

_____

_____

Respect

Think about someone you respect or look up to. It might be someone you are close to, or a person who was there briefly in your life, such as a coach or teacher. What do you feel as you recall them? What memories occur?

Write about what they mean to you and why you respect them. How do their values show up in your life now?

_____

_____

_____

_____

_____

_____

_____

Fictional Role Models

Role models inspire us to do what they do by living by their values, even as they face challenges. We are often drawn to books and movies that show people overcoming adverse events and their own personal limitations by following their value-based goal.

What movies or books were important to you as a child or adolescent? Which character still calls to you? Choose a book or movie with a role model character and read or watch it again. What behaviors demonstrated the character's values? As you reread or watch the story, reflect on what was happening in your life when this person became important to you. Think about how this person influenced your life and values.

Identifying Your Core Values

Values express your deepest wishes about how you want to live in the world. They guide how you want to be with others, with yourself, and in the broader world around you. This exercise will help you sort your values, but you'll need index cards or sticky notes to complete it. Copy the values in the following list onto the cards. If you don't see a value reflected on this list, feel free to add it to a card.

Accepting	Expressive	Mindful
Adventurous	Focused	Open
Assertive	Fair	Orderly
Authentic	Flexible	Persistent
Balance	Friendly	Playful
Beauty	Forgiving	Protective
Caring	Grateful	Respectful
Compassionate	Helpful	Responsible
Cooperative	Honest	Skillful
Courageous	Independent	Supportive
Creative	Industrious	Trusting
Curious	Integrity	Trustworthy
Encouraging	Kind	
Entrepreneurial	Loving	

Go through the stack of values cards and create two piles, one for those you feel a connection to and the other for those you don't.

Now go through the pile of the ones you feel a connection to. If there are more than ten, select the ten that are most important to you.

Go through the stack of ten cards and choose the five most important ones.

Now choose the most important three values. While you rely on many values for guidance, these three are your core values.

What are they? List them on the lines that follow.

_____

_____

_____

What draws you to these values?

_____

_____

_____

Consider posting the cards where you can easily see them or add the words to your life in another way, such as putting them in a screen name or making art with them.

The Cost of Not Living by a Core Value

The times and ways we do not live by our values tend to be very painful. We often avoid thinking about or acknowledging them, even to ourselves.

Choose one of your core values. Describe ways that you live by this value and how that impacts your life. In what ways do you benefit from living by this value?

_____

_____

_____

Now, think about ways in which you do not live by this value. What gets in the way? How is your life impacted by the times and ways you don't uphold this value?

_____

_____

_____

Know Your "Shoulds"

For most of us, the word "should" carries the sense of obligation, loss of freedom, or heaviness. We may feel the desire to flee or to comply when we don't want to. When values are involved, the word or implication of "should" suggests we may be caught in social fusion—when the expectations of others try to override our own dreams and values. This might sound like, "I should value X" or "A smart person would value this networking opportunity, but I want to do Y."

Do you have expectations about what you "should" value that are different from what you want in your heart? Explore how the values you feel obligated to have feel different from those you have for yourself.

From "I Should" to "I Get To"

One way to work with "should" energy, or fusion, is to replace the word "should" with "get to" and notice what you feel. Your emotional or physical response to the change may help you recognize a socially defined value versus a personal value. Complete the table. The first two lines show examples.

I SHOULD	RESPONSE	I GET TO	RESPONSE	VALUES
Make my bed	Heavy. "Ugh, it takes too much energy."	Make my bed	Lighter, more energy. "Yeah, I do get to make my bed and I like how it looks when I do."	Order, tidiness
Cut my hair	Tension, pressure. "My sister will get off my back, if I cut it the way she wants."	Cut my hair	Clarity, sense of self. "Nope, those are her tastes, not mine."	Self-expression

Values in Specific Areas of Your Life

While core values are consistent throughout the various aspects of our lives, we also have values that are specific to the areas or domains of our lives. For example, work values may focus on productivity and achievement, while family values focus on connection and loyalty with an underlying core value of integrity. This subsection will help you explore your values throughout your life.

Exploring Values in Your Life

The following instructions include prompts to help you explore what holds meaning for you in each major area or domain of your life. Some areas may not be important for you and you can leave those blank.

Others may have been impacted by losses in your life; include those. For example, if you've dreamed of running marathons and an injury prevents you, acknowledge the loss and explore what the dreams say about you. "I'm still grieving that I can't run this marathon with my friends, but the underlying hunger tells me that I love vigorous exercise and meeting challenges with friends." You may want to switch to a journal to allow more space for some of the prompts.

Mental, emotional health and growth

- What invites you to be your "best self"?
- What do you respect about yourself?

_____

_____

_____

Physical health

- Describe a time you felt connected to your body.
- What would your ideal relationship with your body look like?

_____

_____

_____

Home

- What makes a living space a home?
- What changes in your home would support you being you?

_____

_____

_____

Leisure/pleasure

- What nonessential activities bring you joy or satisfaction?
- What activities build connection with others, even if you do the activity solo?

_____

_____

_____

Job/career

- What are you proud of in how you do your job?
- Who is helped by your work, even if you never meet them?

_____

_____

_____

Financial

- What helps you feel safe financially?
- What does financial "success" mean to you?

_____

_____

_____

Family—by choice, law, or genetics

- Describe the family members who mean the most to you.
- How would you like them to describe who you are in the relationship?

_____

_____

_____

Romantic partner(s)

- What do you most want in an intimate relationship?
- What do you enjoy giving to or doing for a romantic partner?

_____

_____

_____

Parenting/mentoring

- What qualities do you like to model for the children or young people in your life?
- What behaviors or accomplishments of theirs touch you most deeply?

_____

_____

_____

Friendships

- What attracts you to others as a friend?
- What does "being a good friend" mean to you?

_____

_____

Community/citizenship

- Describe someone you respect for how they give to the community.
- What groups or communities are you a member of?

_____

_____

_____

Spirituality/religion

- What invites a sense of wonder for you?
- Describe a time you shared this sense with another person or a group.

_____

_____

_____

Preparing for death

- What makes for a meaningful death? For example, would dying at home surrounded by loved ones deepen your family's ties? Or would dying within a hospice residence protect your loved ones?
- What rituals and services have helped you after someone died?

_____

_____

Identifying Key Values in Each Domain

The prior activity, Exploring Values in Your Life, may have helped you begin to identify which values are most important in the various domains of your life. In this activity, you will do a values card sort for the domains you choose.

On index cards or small pieces of paper, write out a deck of your values, use the values on page 151 for assistance. Choose an area of life you want to work on and sort the cards into piles of Very Important, Important, and Not Important for this domain. Write your values for the domains in the boxes.

AREA/DOMAIN	CARD	VERY IMPORTANT	IMPORTANT	NOT IMPORTANT
Mental, emotional health and growth				
Physical health				
Home				
Leisure, pleasure				
Job/career				
Financial				
Family—by choice, law, or genetics				
Romantic partner(s)				
Parenting/ mentoring				
Friendships				
Community/ citizenship				
Spirituality/religion				
Preparing for death				

Where Are You Now?

1. Pick eight life areas that you want to focus on using the previous chart. If you prefer to do more or fewer, you can modify as needed.

2. Label each line with one of your focus areas.

3. Add up to three of your key values for each area.

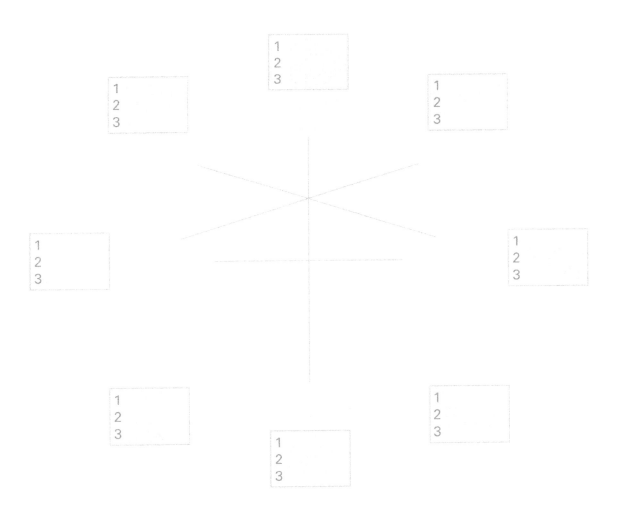

4. Choose a domain to start with. Mark on the line how close you are now to living by those values.

5. Mark where you would like to be for that domain.

6. Repeat for each of the domains you choose.

7. Connect the where-you-are-now marks. Color the section from the center to this line.

8. What do you notice about where you are? Describe your experience of acknowledging where you are.

_____

_____

_____

_____

9. Connect the where-I-want-to-be marks. Color the section from the where-I-am-now line to this new line.

10. Reflect on what it is like to see the variations in how much you are living by your values now.

_____

_____

_____

_____

Applying Your Values to Death

Death is one of the most difficult aspects of life to accept. Most of us find ways to avoid thinking about it or find ourselves ruminating about it in unhelpful ways. Exploring how to approach death with your values in mind can help you find more peace with this challenging reality.

Choose someone you can explore this exercise with. Think about whether you want a more personal discussion or to gather information. Talking with friends or family members about those you have lost and what that experience was like for each of you is one option. Another approach would be to contact a professional such as a hospice counselor, spiritual leader, or mortuary professional. Consider topics such as dying at home versus in a hospice or hospital, whether to have a funeral or celebration of life, how one can show their love even after they are gone.

The purpose of these conversations is to explore how approaching death through the lens of your values can help you be more present in your life.

Money

Money is so much more than a currency for purchasing material items and experiences. Money is often fused with the expression of love or with personal worth. Managing money well involves understanding how to budget and save, to plan, and whether and how to invest. For most of us, money requires finding and keeping a job. In ACT vocabulary, our experiences with money tend to create significant fusions and with them, psychological rigidity. In this exercise, journal about how money plays a role in your life. What values do you have about it and the impact it has on the lives of so many? Consider writing about your parents' or guardians' values and behaviors around money and how you were impacted by them. In what ways are you living by your financial values? And in what ways are you not living by them?

_____

_____

_____

_____

_____

_____

_____

_____

_____

_____

Discuss Values with Someone Important to You

Having and discussing shared values helps improve the quality of relationships. Just as values help guide our personal choices, they also help guide relationships in ways that work for both of you. Knowing where our values overlap, and where they don't, can help define and improve a relationship.

Think about someone important to you that you'd like to discuss your respective values with. You might choose a romantic partner or child, a sibling or parent, a friend or colleague. How do values show up in this particular relationship? Think about what you would like to explore with them. Are you more interested in exploring values with them or resolving a conflict based on different values? Would you like to find values in common or discuss those that differ? Are you interested in learning how they developed a given value and what it means to them?

Choosing to Live by Your Values in the Moment

Choices that invite us to live by our values show up throughout the day. When we are living in the present, we have a better chance of noticing the choices. Do I hit the snooze button and sleep longer or let it ring so it helps me get out of bed on time? Do I work an extra hour at work or go home to be with the family? Each of these seemingly small choices allows us to choose which of our values to live by.

How do your values show up in this day-to-day manner? What interferes or makes it difficult to allow a value to guide your choice? Last, what helps you choose when values are in conflict?

_____

_____

_____

_____

_____

_____

_____

_____

_____

When We Must Choose Between Values

Some of the more difficult times in our lives occur when we must choose between values. This can occur when we need to choose between completing a work assignment or taking care of ourselves or another. When we are caregivers for one person in our lives, it can mean we have less time for other important people and activities in our lives. Falling into a pattern of sacrificing the same value and area repeatedly can happen easily.

What are situations where you feel pulled between two important values? How do you tend to resolve it? What are the costs and benefits of your choices?

_____

_____

_____

_____

_____

_____

_____

_____

_____

_____

_____

What Would Change If You Live More Fully by a Core Value?

Go back over your core values as well as those for each domain. Does one value stand out as the more defining value of your life? In what domains does it show up?

_____

_____

_____

What is important to you about this value?

_____

_____

_____

In what ways do you currently live by this value?

_____

_____

_____

When and how do you not live by this value?

_____

_____

_____

What is your internal experience when you do not live by this value?

Thoughts

_____

_____

_____

Feelings

_____

_____

_____

Sensations

_____

_____

_____

Behavioral urges

_____

_____

_____

What, if any, unwanted behaviors do you engage in if you don't live by this value?

_____

_____

_____

How would your life change if you were able to commit to living more often and fully by this value?

_____

_____

_____

Key Takeaways

Our values are important because they help us be the person we most want to be in the world, for ourselves and others. We make hundreds of decisions every day that create our present and our future possibilities. Knowing what's important to us helps us make decisions based on those values and to move toward living a more purposeful life.

✓ Personal values express who and how we want to be in the world.

✓ Social fusion can create false values that we believe we "ought" to have.

✓ Core values express our hearts' deepest desires and can guide us in many areas of our lives.

✓ The different areas of our lives have specific values appropriate to the needs of that area.

✓ Major areas to help us develop our values in life include: mental, emotional health and growth, physical health, home, leisure/pleasure, job/career, financial, family, romantic partner(s), parenting/mentoring, friendships, community/citizenship, spirituality/religion, preparing for death. Knowing our values increases our ability to make values-based decisions moment by moment.

CHAPTER 8

Acting and Behaving in Accordance with Your Values

Ytou have learned many tools in this workbook to dismantle the grip of depression: defusion techniques, acceptance, being present, unraveling sticky patterns, and identifying your values. In this chapter, you integrate those skills with committed action toward creating a purposeful life. The first section offers tools to help you identify dreams and build action plans for bringing them into reality. The second section guides you in building a wellness plan to identify and address signs of depression to prevent a recurrence. The last section helps you assess your growth and strengthen your commitment to continued actionable healing.

Committing to Face Hidden Depression

KAREN WAS A SINGLE MOTHER of four adult children and a highly valued manager at a credit union. She worked long hours and prided herself on being reliable. Her social life was active, and she said her vivaciousness kept people seeking her out. She'd learned early to be there for others without expecting much in return. She knew how to keep people smiling to avoid conflict but felt lonely and paralyzed because she kept everyone, even her children, at arm's length. Her pattern was to push hard until she crashed and hibernated for days to weeks, then to start the cycle over.

Karen came to therapy after learning that her daughter had not told her about an important breakup in her life or that she had gone to the hospital for depression after the breakup. She did not want her daughter to struggle alone as she had all of her life. Her son supported his sister's decision to keep challenging events away from her, saying they both loved Karen and did not want to send her into a hibernation period. Her therapy goals were to be able to slow down without sinking into a stagnating depression and to be closer to her children emotionally.

She had never told them or anyone about her father's drunken rages and physical abuse, or how she married their father to escape only to learn he had similar patterns. Never mentioned that when she "hibernated" she was often lying on the floor in abject despair. She could see how her periodic disappearances affected her children and how similar patterns were playing out in their lives and relationships. She needed to heal those relationships and help them have more satisfying lives than she had.

Karen struggled with being present and with permitting herself to experience the emotions she felt about her past and its impact on her children. She was more comfortable being "fine" until she wasn't. Karen's core values were honesty and helping her children have more satisfying lives than she had. Committing to actions based on these values helped her accept more of her own experience and open the door to learning more about her children's experiences. She committed to counseling with her children and they began working on connecting more deeply.

Committing to a Life Beyond Depression

This section helps you develop dreams and action plans to build a life based on the values you identified in each relevant area of your life.

Dreaming the Life You Want

What would you like your life to be like five years from now? What relationships might change or be left behind? What relationships might be added? Will your source of income be more in alignment with your values? What changes would you like in your self-care, your living space?

Using the graphic, write one of your values in the center image. Think about all the life changes that might take place if you live by this value over the next five years and write them in the surrounding images. The example that follows shows how Jorge wants to integrate his value of beauty into his life more fully.

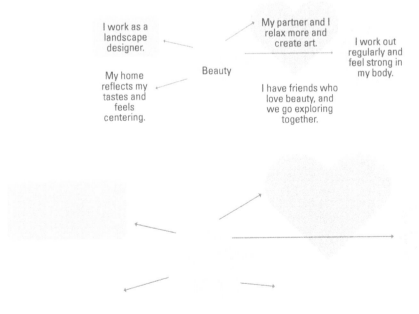

Creating a Vision Board

The classic adage "a picture paints a thousand words" is especially true when it comes to creating a purposeful life. Images awaken possibilities. Vision boards combine images and inspiring words with intentions to help you imagine a dream more fully. If you did the last exercise, Dreaming the Life You Want, you could continue to work with that value and how it might show up in your life.

Choose one or more of your dreams for your vision board. It might be a physical dream, such as a new home where you could live your value of creating safety and comfort to support your family, or an internal dream, such as living with a sense of peace in several domains of your life. Decide whether you want to create a physical or online vision board.

Collect items for your vision board: images, color or pattern swatches, words or quotes that inspire you.

When you are ready, set aside some time for making your board. You may want to practice mindfulness before you start. Some people enjoy listening to music. You may want one or more friends to join you or you may prefer to be alone.

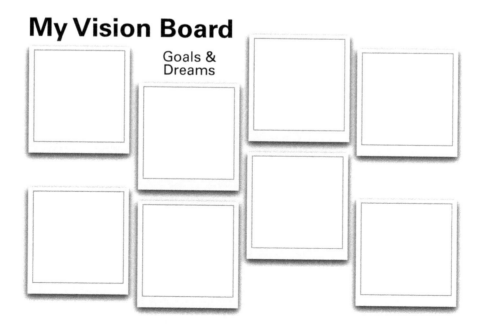

My Vision Board

Goals & Dreams

Defusing from Behaviors and Memories until You Are Ready to Address Them

Choosing which life-affirming changes to start with includes choosing the behaviors and life situations you will not yet tackle. For example, you might decide to stop drinking before quitting smoking. Or you might feel ready to experience the loss of a longtime friend but not yet the impact of a health condition.

Sometimes it is enough to name that you will address the other items in their time. Other times, the negative thoughts and emotions about the tasks you have deferred can continue to assail you. Imagining a container to place them in can help.

For this practice, allow yourself to experience the negative thoughts surrounding the need to delay a change, and then guide them into an imaginary container. The container can be any size or shape you find works. Add locks if they are helpful.

If you decided to organize the pantry before the garage, you might have the negative thoughts, "I am such a loser that my home is so disorganized. I need those items in the garage now. I can't wait until the pantry is done."

You could respond, "Hello thoughts. Thank you for reminding me how much you miss the items in the garage. For now, you need to wait in this chest so I can complete my first goal."

Imagine the thoughts and stress going into the chest. See whether they will stay there or if you need a lock. Reassure the thoughts and feelings that you will be back for them, that this is temporary to give you time to complete the first task. You may want to write the thoughts down and put them in a box or place to be reviewed later.

Setting SMART Goals

George Doran developed the SMART goal-setting approach to help people define realistic goals. The approach has been integrated into many areas, including educational and therapeutic arenas, including ACT. I've modified the SMART goals a little bit to fit the needs of this workbook.

Specific: Write goals that include details, such as how often, when, where.
Measurable: Plan how you will know whether you met your goal.
Attainable: Choose goals that are doable, given the realities of your life.
Relevant: Set values-based goals that get you closer to your dreams.
Time-framed: Set a date and time by which a goal will be met.

SMART GOAL SETTING GUIDE				
S SPECIFIC	**M** MEASURABLE	**A** ATTAINABLE	**R** RELEVANT	**T** TIME-FRAMED
What do I want to accomplish? How often do I do it? Who is involved? What requirements are there?	How often, how much? Measurement unit (minutes, outcome, etc.)	How can this goal be accomplished? What barriers might show up? How realistic is the goal given constraints? What modifications can make it more attainable?	What values are connected with this goal? How will these values show up as you work on this goal? How does this get you closer to your dream?	How does this get you closer to your dream? Is this a one-time task or one that is recurrent? If it is recurrent, how often will you complete it?

Breaking Your Goal into Steps

Planning out the steps of a values-based committed action plan increases the likelihood of completing the plan, and in the time frame and budget you want. This exercise helps you break down an action plan into manageable steps and walks you through an example using Jorge's goal of integrating his value of beauty into his life more.

The steps of a committed action plan often fit into an outline form. For example, if the plan is to reduce your debt, an outline might include a high-level task such as developing a budget. The next level task might include identifying how much money you receive each month and what bills you must pay.

1. Define your goal in the context of the value(s) it supports.

    Choose one of the goals you've explored in an earlier activity or define a new one.
    Jorge chose to focus on having his home reflect his tastes more and defined the specific goal of creating a garden section that included bright-colored vegetables he enjoyed cooking with. He wants to complete the preparations within a month to meet the growing cycles for some of the plants.

2. Name what you need to complete the goal. If you need to learn more about what you need, add that as the first high-level step.

    Jorge identified needing plants, prepared soil, and researched information about how to maintain the plants during their growth cycle.

3. Identify high-level steps to achieving this.

    Jorge identified choosing the plants he wanted, preparing the soil, determining the watering and fertilizing schedule required, and planting the plants with any structure they needed.

4. Break the first high-level step into smaller steps. You can do the others or wait until you have made progress on the first step.

   Jorge set the steps of talking with his grandfather about the plants to choose and getting seedlings from him, buying fertilizer, preparing the soil, buying additional plants, and planting.

5. Schedule the high and lower-level steps.

   Jorge scheduled his activities around his work schedule and other commitments.

Now it's your turn:

1. Define your goal: choose one of the goals you've explored in an earlier activity or define a new one.

   _____

   _____

   _____

   _____

2. Name what you need to complete the goal. If you need to learn more about what you need, add that as the first high-level step.

   _____

   _____

   _____

   _____

3. Identify high-level steps.

_____

_____

_____

_____

4. Break the high-level steps into smaller steps.

_____

_____

_____

_____

5. Schedule the high and lower-level steps.

_____

_____

_____

_____

Visualizing Success

Visualizing our success as a goal, large or small, increases the likelihood we will complete the goal and on time. Choose one of your goals and write about the moment you will complete the goal. What might you see? What will it feel like? Who, if anyone, will be with you? If fears or concerns arise, write those as well and see whether the image of your success changes to address them.

_____

_____

_____

_____

_____

_____

_____

_____

_____

_____

_____

Committed Action Worksheet

Life does not stop happening because of our plans. We can count on internal and external obstacles to show up along the way. This exercise invites you to prepare for the ones you can foresee. Write down a step you plan to take and identify any obstacles that might arise. Then list how you might work with the obstacles.

The first step of an example for Jorge is shown.

My Values: Increasing the beauty in my life and the world
Goal: I want to complete a certification program in landscape design.
Domains this goal affects: Purposeful work
Dream this goal supports: Becoming a landscape designer

STEPS	OBSTACLES	TOOLS	DATES COMPLETED
1. Find a program through an online search.	Hopelessness, sense of failure	2. Accept my feelings (These Feelings Belong, page 76) 3. Visualize graduating	
	Some websites are overwhelming.	1. Set up an appointment with the tech support at the library.	

My Values: _____

_____

Goal: _____

_____

Domains this goal affects: _____

_____

Dream this goal supports: _____

_____

STEPS	OBSTACLES	TOOLS	DATES COMPLETED

Share One of Your Commitments

Defining your values and committing to living by them through specific actions is a transformative piece of work. The next step is sharing them. Taking the commitment beyond ourselves can mean telling a single trusted person, accepting a role in a community, or making a promise to the person we are committed to helping.

Choose how you will share your commitment. Make any necessary arrangements. Journaling can help you identify barriers and plan around them.

Once you have shared your committed action, take time to journal about it. Include what went well and any challenges that arose. Reviewing these important steps creates space to notice that you are living by your values and how you can get even better at doing so.

Creating a Wellness and Recovery Action Plan

The Wellness and Recovery Action Plan (WRAP), originally developed by author and educator Mary Ellen Copeland, is a well researched and proven practice for recovery from mental health challenges including depression. The plan helps you track your psychological flexibility status from when you are doing well to the first signs of distress, when things are breaking down and when you need someone else to intervene.

At each stage, you identify what will help you stay healthy or return to health. People who use a WRAP plan have been able to reduce or eliminate their time lost to depression and hospitalizations for depression.

This section will help guide you in developing your own Wellness and Recovery Action Plan while integrating the ACT tools with other tools you find useful. For a downloadable template for WRAP, see the Resources section on page 204.

Lapse versus Relapse

Maintaining new life-affirming habits requires noticing when the habits start to slip and deciding to choose them again. If you notice them quickly and make the necessary changes, you can turn the lapse in healthy habits around and prevent a full relapse from occurring. You can also notice the early onset of symptoms when life stressors increase or your support decreases, at which point you can increase your healthy habits or external support.

What early signs of depression do you experience? What helps you notice them? Write about a time you were able to recognize an increase in depression symptoms and make an adjustment that helped you have a better day.

_____

_____

_____

_____

_____

_____

_____

_____

_____

_____

_____

Wellness Toolbox

This activity will have you identify tools to help you stay, or return to being, centered and well. Check off the ones you have tried and star any that you found particularly helpful. Add items that aren't included, as you discover them.

Acceptance Tools

☐ These Feelings Belong (page 76)

Calming Tools

☐ Moving with Your Breath (page 101)

☐ coloring or handiwork

Defusion Tools

☐ Sound Play (page 38)

☐ Remote Control (page 39)

☐ talking with a receptive listener

Energizing Tools

☐ Breathing to Energize (page 92)

☐ exercise

Here and Now Tools

☐ Grounding in Sound (page 91)

☐ Moving with Your Breath (page 101)

☐ use your "grounding kit" (page 104) if you've made one

Other

Daily Maintenance Plan

The daily maintenance plan lists the things you need to do on a daily, weekly, and monthly basis to stay healthy or in the zone. The first step is to describe yourself when you are doing well and what life patterns help you stay well.

What are you like when you are doing well? Include specific behaviors that will help people who know you, and those who don't, recognize whether you are doing well.

_____

_____

How would a close friend or family member describe you when you are doing well?

_____

_____

What do you need to do on a daily basis to continue doing well?

TIME	WELLNESS ACTIVITIES
Morning	
Afternoon	
Evening	
Sleep protocol	

What do you need to do on a weekly basis?

_____

_____

_____

_____

_____

What do you need to do on a monthly basis?

_____

_____

_____

_____

_____

Identifying Your Key Stressors

Knowing the external events that are likely to increase your stress level can help you plan steps to regain your psychological flexibility. In the table, add the specific stressor you experience for each category and the tools that can help you return to center.

CATEGORY	MY STRESSORS	WHAT TO DO
Relationship with partner or absence of one		
Physical pain		
Health issues or limits		
Family relationships		
Reminders of painful events		
Work or school		
Money/finances		
Regrets about past behavior or choices		
Other		

Early Warning Signs

Identify the early warning signs in each category.

Thoughts	Feelings
Sensations	Urges and behaviors

What will help you address these patterns before they get worse. What tools have you learned in this workbook that will help you?

_____

_____

_____

_____

Who would you like to receive help from?

_____

_____

_____

_____

When Things Are Breaking Down

When depression is significantly impacting your life, what changes in each category?

Thoughts	Feelings
Sensations	Urges and behaviors

What behavior or skill will help you address these patterns before they worsen?

_____

_____

_____

Who can you go to for additional support?

_____

_____

_____

Naming Your No

Part of finding what works is surviving what does not. What treatment experiences have you gone through that either didn't work or were harmful? It may be medications that came with frightening or unacceptable side effects, clinicians who left you feeling worse, or treatment programs where you felt or were unsafe. Write about the mental health treatment experiences that have been difficult for you.

_____

_____

_____

_____

_____

_____

_____

_____

_____

_____

_____

_____

Crisis Plan

The crisis plan is a stand-alone section that you can provide clinicians and crisis staff so that they know your crisis treatment preferences.

Part 1: What I'm like when I'm well.

You can use the description you completed for the Daily Maintenance section (page 189).

_____

_____

Part 2: Describe what indicates that you need crisis support.

_____

_____

Part 3: Provide the names, contact details, and description of those who support you. If you would like your clinician to be able to speak with anyone, you will need to provide written permission for them to do so. You can specify limits on what they may say.

NAME	CONTACT INFO	ROLE	PERMISSION TO SPEAK

Part 4: List medications that have been helpful and those that have been problematic.

MEDICATION	HELPFUL	NOT HELPFUL	UNWANTED EFFECT

Part 5: List any treatments and complimentary therapies you have found helpful and not helpful.

TREATMENT TYPE	HELPFUL	NOT HELPFUL	UNWANTED EFFECT

Part 6: Identify any home and community care available to you.
For example, if you've felt unsafe to stay alone at home while you attended a full-day treatment program, who could you stay with or have stay with you until you felt able to stay alone?

_____

_____

_____

Part 7: List your preferred treatment facilities and those you are unwilling to go to.

_____

_____

_____

Part 8: It helps to define what you want to happen after the crisis is over. Describe how and when to inactivate the crisis plan, as well as naming the support you would like post-crisis.

_____

_____

_____

Sharing Your WRAP Selectively

Think about who you would like to share part or all of your WRAP (see page 186) with. You may want to give a copy to the family, friends, or professional helpers you want to be part of turning increased symptoms around. You may want to give them permission to speak with one another, and you will want to establish the limits of what each can say to whom.

Although a WRAP is not a legal document, clinicians and ER staff will often consider your preferences in a crisis situation. Developing and sharing your WRAP is preparing for the worst situation while living for the best.

This week, choose at least one person to share your WRAP with and explain why it's important. You may want to first ask them if they are comfortable with the type of support you'd like from them, and thank them for being part of your team.

Celebrating Your Work

Putting your dreams into action to create a rich and purposeful life is well worth celebrating, and this section will help you appreciate the progress you have made.

Post-Traumatic Growth Inventory

We grow and heal as we come to terms with our lives and the difficult experiences we have experienced. Richard Tedeschi and Lawrence Calhoun (1996) developed the Post-Traumatic Growth Inventory that identifies five areas of growth after experiencing a traumatic event: Personal Strength, New Possibilities, Improved Relationships, Spiritual Growth, and Appreciation for Life. The scale measures growth after losses and conditions including depression.

On the inventory table, rate each statement for how true it feels for you now, 0 means not at all true and 5 means extremely true.

STATEMENTS	0	1	2	3	4	5
1. I changed my priorities about what is important in life.						
2. I have a greater appreciation for the value of my own life.						
3. I have developed new interests.						
4. I have a greater feeling of self-reliance.						
5. I have a better understanding of spiritual matters.						
6. I more clearly see that I can count on people in times of trouble.						
7. I established a new path for my life.						
8. I have a greater sense of closeness with others.						
9. I am more willing to express my emotions.						

STATEMENTS	0	1	2	3	4	5
10. I know that I can handle difficulties.						
11. I can do better things with my life.						
12. I am better able to accept the way things work out.						
13. I can better appreciate each day.						
14. New opportunities are available which wouldn't have been otherwise.						
15. I have more compassion for others.						
16. I put more effort into my relationships.						
17. I am more likely to try to change things that need changing.						
18. I have stronger religious faith.						
19. I discovered that I'm stronger than I thought I was.						
20. I learned a great deal about how wonderful people are.						
21. I better accept needing others.						

The statements are grouped in the table by the area of growth. Add your points for each area and divide by the number of questions for that area (shown in parentheses by the name) to get the average of your growth in that area. In what areas have you experienced growth?

FACTOR ITEM	NUMBERS
Personal strength (4)	4, 10, 12, 19
New possibilities (5)	3, 7, 11, 14, 17
Improved relationships (7)	6, 8, 9, 15, 16, 20, 21
Spiritual growth (2)	5, 18
Appreciation for life (3)	1, 2, 13

Appreciating Where You Are Now

Think about the ways your life has changed since you began working with the ACT model. What are you most proud of? What surprises you about the choices you have made and are making?

_____

_____

_____

_____

_____

_____

_____

_____

_____

_____

_____

_____

Key Takeaways

This chapter was meant to support you in linking your dreams to your values and then transforming the dreams into committed, actionable items. In addition to helping you define the committed actions for living a life beyond depression, the steps for establishing a plan for how to manage your depression (including one you can share with others when you are in crisis and your team who will support you through it) were covered.

✓ Identifying dreams based on your values is the first step in creating a purposeful life.

✓ Developing SMART (Specific, Measurable, Attainable, Relevant, Time-framed) goals and breaking them down into small steps helps you achieve them.

✓ Creating Committed Action Plans helps you keep track of your progress.

✓ The Wellness and Recovery Action Plan (WRAP) is your personal plan for preventing and managing a recurrence of depression.

✓ Celebrate your moments of living in the zone in a life rich with purpose and vitality.

MOVING FORWARD WITH ACCEPTANCE, COMMITMENT, AND HOPE

Congratulations on the important work you have done to complete this workbook. Although we haven't met in person, I am smiling as I think of you at this stage of your journey. What activities and ideas did you find most helpful to you? Which practices have you now integrated into your life? What did you learn about yourself that surprised you?

You have shown impressive commitment to completing this book and I commend you. In finishing it, you have lived your dedication to pursuing a purposeful life, to being present to the now, and to facing many of the painful emotions and experiences that were simpler to avoid.

Learning how to practice the psychological skills of ACT—defusion, acceptance, shifting from the conceptualized-self to self-as-context, living in the present, defining values, and defining committed action plans to create the values-based life you most want—is the biggest and most challenging part of changing your life. And it is the first step to living by these skills the rest of your life.

Life brings us new challenges regularly. When new challenges show up in your life, reviewing the skills you learned here may help you in ways that keep you focused on being the you that you most want to be.

RESOURCES

Anxiety & Depression Association of America (ADAA): adaa.org

Association for Contextual Behavioral Science: contextualscience.org/act

Debtors Anonymous: debtorsanonymous.org

Depression and Bipolar Support Alliance (DBSA): dbsalliance.org

Fidget toys and sensory aides: sensorytoyshop.com/sensory-products
-44-c.asp

My Healthy Place: healthyplace.com/depression/articles/about-mary
-ellen-copeland

National Alliance on Mental Health (NAMI): nami.org

The National Suicide Prevention Lifeline (available 24/7): (800) 273-TALK (8255)

Psychosocial Recovery and Rehabilitation (PRR): verywellmind.com
/psychosocial-rehabilitation-4589796.

Substance Abuse and Mental Health Services Administration (SAMHSA):
samhsa.gov

Weighted blankets (reviews): buyersguide.org/weighted-blanket/t/best.

Wellness Recovery Action Plan (WRAP) download: namirockland.org
/uploads/3/4/0/3/34038357/blank_wrap_forms_with_mc_permission.pdf

REFERENCES

Bai, Zhenggang, Shiga Luo, Luyao Zhang, Sijie Wu, and Iris Chi. "Acceptance and commitment therapy (ACT) to reduce depression: A systematic review and meta-analysis." *Journal of Affective Disorders* 260 (2020): 728–737. doi.org/10.1016/j.jad.2019.09.040.

Buckner, Randy L., Jessica R. Andrews-Hanna, and Daniel L. Schacter. "The brain's default network: anatomy, function, and relevance to disease." *Annals of the New York Academy of Sciences* 1124, no. 1 (2008): 1–38. doi.org/10.1196/annals.1440.011.

Doran, George T. "There's a S.M.A.R.T. way to write management's goals and objectives." *Management Review* 70, no. 11 (1981): 35–36.

Evans, Wyatt R., Robyn D. Walser, Kent D. Drescher, and Jacob K. Farnsworth. *The Moral Injury Workbook: Acceptance and Commitment Therapy Skills for Moving Beyond Shame, Anger, and Trauma to Reclaim Your Values*. Oakland, CA: New Harbinger Publications, 2020.

Guan, Naijie, Alessandra Guariglia, Patrick Moore, Fangzhou Xu, and Hareth Al-Janabi. "Financial stress and depression in adults: A systematic review." *PloS one* 17, no. 2 (2022). doi.org/10.1371/journal.pone.0264041.

Howard, David M., Mark J. Adams, Toni-Kim Clarke, Jonathan D. Hafferty, Jude Gibson, Masoud Shirali, Jonathan R. I. Coleman, et al. "Genome-wide meta-analysis of depression identifies 102 independent variants and highlights the importance of the prefrontal brain regions." *Nature Neuroscience* 22, no. 3 (2019): 343–352. doi.org/10.1038/s41593-018-0326-7.

Nummenmaa, Lauri, Enrico Glerean, Riitta Hari, and Jari K. Hietanen. "Bodily maps of emotions." *Proceedings of the National Academy of Sciences* 111, no. 2 (2014): 646–651. pubmed.ncbi.nlm.nih.gov/24379370.

Rytwinski, Nina K., Michael D. Scur, Norah C. Feeny, and Eric A. Youngstrom. "The co-occurrence of major depressive disorder among individuals with posttraumatic stress disorder: A meta-analysis." *Journal of Traumatic Stress* 26, no. 3 (2013): 299–309. doi.org/10.1002/jts.21814.

Sanada, Kenji, Shinichiro Nakajima, Shunya Kurokawa, Alberto Barceló-Soler, Daisuke Ikuse, Akihito Hirata, Akira Yoshizawa, et al. "Gut microbiota and major depressive disorder: A systematic review and meta-analysis." *Journal of Affective Disorders* 266 (2020): 1–13. doi.org/10.1016/j.jad.2020.01.102.

Tedeschi, Richard G., and Lawrence G. Calhoun. "The Posttraumatic Growth Inventory: Measuring the positive legacy of trauma." *Journal of Traumatic Stress* 9, no. 3 (1996): 455–471. doi.org/10.1007/BF02103658.

Tirch, D., Schoendorff, B., and Silberstein, L. R. *The ACT Practitioner's Guide to the Science of Compassion: Tools for Fostering Psychological Flexibility.* Oakland, CA: New Harbinger Publications, 2014.

Wells, Adrian, and Peter Fisher, eds. *Treating Depression: MCT, CBT, and Third Wave Therapies.* Hoboken, NJ: John Wiley & Sons, 2015.

INDEX

Acknowledgments

First and foremost, thank you to my beloved daughter, Dakoda, for being patient and supportive when I wrote during weekends and evenings.

Deep thanks belong to the many patients whose honest feedback about what helped and what did not deepened my appreciation of and skills with delivering ACT.

Robyn Walser, my first ACT instructor, who warmly demonstrated the power and fun of inviting transformation through ACT.

Richard Williams, colleague and author, who encouraged and consulted with me during the development of this book.

Special thanks to the editors who helped this book come into being: Rakhshan Rizwan, Mo Mozuch, and Yasmin McClinton.

About the Author

 **Elizabeth Weiss, PsyD,** is a clinical psychologist in the San Francisco Bay Area. She specializes in helping people overcome challenging circumstances to live full, satisfying lives. She is a participant in the 2022 cohort of the Applied Compassion Training at Stanford University and looks forward to bringing more compassion to the issues of depression and mental health.

CPSIA information can be obtained
at www.ICGtesting.com
Printed in the USA
JSHW041532290623
43865JS00001B/2